DESCARTES DICTIONARY

DESCARTES
DICTIONARY

Translated and Edited by

JOHN M. MORRIS
KIRKLAND COLLEGE

PHILOSOPHICAL LIBRARY

New York

Copyright, 1971, by Philosophical Library, Inc.,
15 East 40 Street, New York, New York 10016

Library of Congress Catalog Card No. 73-137789

SBN 8022-2046-0

Manufactured in the United States of America

PREFACE

The purpose of this *Descartes Dictionary* is to bring together as many as possible of the technical and special terms in Descartes' writings with their definitions in Descartes' own words. Not all of the entries are explicit definitions, although most of them are; there are also implicit characterizations of the meanings of many words, and a handful of entries were included simply for their own sake—because Descartes had something interesting to say about his life and world.

All of the entries, or almost all of them, have been newly translated for this volume. (The exceptions are a half-dozen of the passages in the *Rules* and most of the *Notes against a Program*, which were taken from the Haldane-Ross translation.) There are many reasons for preparing new translations: The language in the older translations is archaic and often inaccurate; many of Descartes' most important works have never been translated into English; and modern translations vary in quality and style. What is most important, though, is just that the old Haldane-Ross translation simply failed to pay attention to the technical language that Descartes used, and so blurred some of the most important distinctions that he made. To cite just one example (one of the most glaring ones), on two pages of the Haldane-Ross translation, various forms of the French word *connaissance* are given six different translations into English: recognize, understand, knowledge, cognizance, apprehend, and comprehend (pp. 92-93). The English-speaking reader has no way of telling that this assortment of words all refers back to the same French (and Latin) concept—knowledge by acquaintance or recognition.

The translations used here, then, are specifically intended to throw some light on Descartes' own vocabulary, and they are as literal as it was possible to make them, without sacrificing readability. The French versions of the *Meditations* and the *Principles of Philosophy* were used, rather than the Latin, because Descartes himself revised and approved these translations, and some of the changes that he made are significant.

None of the passages has been condensed, but many of them appear as parts of longer sentences. Leading words have often been deleted, and the endings of many of Descartes' long sentences have been omitted. Sometimes a word or two has been added, to make a passage more intelligible; these additions are enclosed in brackets.

Following each listing, the source from which it was drawn is named, together with the section number, if it has one. Then follow the volume and page numbers of the standard Adam and Tannery edition of the works of Descartes (except for a few passages from works that do not appear in the AT edition).

Students using this dictionary will find that it gives some needed clarifications of the terms that Descartes introduces into his writings without explanation—terms like *animal spirits, common notions, natural light,* and so on—and for which he gives definitions or explanations only in his letters, or in some obscure, unpublished work. Of course use of the dictionary is no substitute for a close study of the texts themselves; all of these brief passages are wrenched from their context, and many of them can be misleading (or unintelligible) without some understanding of the purposes that they serve in the Cartesian system, a system that depends heavily upon method and order. But for someone who has accepted Descartes' invitation to spend some weeks or months in meditation with him upon the basis of human knowledge and the search for truth, the dictionary may provide some assistance.

Finally, many of the entries were included specifically for the general reader, who would like to hear some of the things that Descartes had to say about people and the world. A gentleman soldier himself, he wrote to men of the world, and to a queen and a princess, attempting to show that his philosophical method applied to practical affairs.

My thanks to Theresa McCracken and Kathy Morris for alphabetizing the entries, and, not infrequently, for correcting my spelling.

John M. Morris

DESCARTES CHRONOLOGY

1596 — Birth of Descartes at La Haye.

1606 — Enters college at La Flèche.

1614 — Leaves La Flèche, studies law at Poitiers.

1616 — Graduates from Poitiers.

1618 — Soldier under Maurice of Orange. *Compendium Musicae* (unpublished).

1619 — Nov. 10: Dreams mark turning-point in vocation.

1620 — Travels in Europe. *Cogitationes Privatae, Olympica* (unpublished).

1628 — *Rules for the Direction of the Mind* (uncompleted, unpublished).

1633 — Condemnation of Galileo. *The World* and *Treatise on Man* prepared for publication but withdrawn.

1637 — *Discourse on Method, Dioptrics, Geometry, Meteorology,* first published work.

1640 — Death of Descartes' daughter and father.

1641 — *Meditations,* with *Objections,* and *Replies.*

1644 — *Principles of Philosophy.*

1645 — *Search for Truth* (unpublished, date uncertain).

1647 — *Notes against a Program* published without Descartes' permission. *Discourse on the Human Body* (unfinished, unpublished, as were other anatomical works).

1648 — Interview with Burman.

1649 — *Passions of the Soul* published. *Birth of Peace,* a ballet on the Peace of Westphalia written for the Queen of Sweden.

1650 — Death of Descartes in Sweden.

DESCARTES' WRITINGS IN ENGLISH TRANSLATION

Philosophical Works of Descartes, Elizabeth S. Haldane and G. R. T. Ross, translators, New York, Dover Publications, 1955, (reprint of 1931 edition).

Rules for the Direction of the Mind, Laurence J. Lafleur, translator, Indianapolis, Bobbs-Merrill, 1961.

Discourse, Optics, Geometry, Meteorology, Paul J. Olscamp, translator, Indianapolis, Bobbs-Merrill, 1965.

(The *Discourse* and the *Meditations* are available in many modern translations.)

Descartes: Philosophical Letters, Anthony Kenny, translator, Oxford, Clarendon Press, 1970.

Volume and page references following each entry refer to the standard edition of Descartes' works, *Oeuvres de Descartes,* edited by Charles Adam & Paul Tannery, Paris, Cerf, 1897-1913; 13 vols. Reprinted in part, with corrections, Vrin, 1957-   .

Additional selections were taken from *Descartes: Oeuvres Philosophiques,* Ferdinand Alquié, editor, Paris, Garnier, 1963-   ; 3 vols.

Birth of Peace appears in "Un Ballet de Descartes," by Albert Thibaudet and Johan Nordström, *Revue de Genève,* vol. I (1920), pp. 163-185.

A

ABSOLUTE

I call "absolute" everything which contains in itself, in the pure and simple state, the nature with which we are concerned: such as everything which is considered as independent, cause, simple, universal, one, equal, similar, straight, or orther qualities like this; and I apply the term "absolute" to the simplest and easiest, because of the use that we make of it in the resolution of our questions.

Rules, VI. X, 381-382

◈   ◈   ◈

See *relative*.

ABSTRACTION

There is a great difference [between *distinction* and *abstraction*], for in distinguishing a substance from its accidents one ought to consider each separately, which greatly helps in knowing it; if, instead, one separates a substance from its accidents solely by abstraction, that is, if one considers it all alone without thinking of them, that prevents one from knowing it as well, because it is by the accidents that the nature of the substance is manifested.

Letter to Clerselier. IX, 217.

◈   ◈   ◈

To find out whether my idea is rendered incomplete, or *inadaequata*, by some abstraction of my mind, I simply examine whether I have derived it, not from some external object which is more complete, but from some other idea which I have myself, which is more ample or complete, and this *per abstractionem intellectus*, i.e., by turning my thought from what is comprised in that more ample idea, in order to apply it better and to make myself more attentive to the other part.

Letter to Gibieuf, Jan. 19, 1642.
III, 474-475.

❖ ❖ ❖

There is a great difference between *abstraction* and *exclusion*. If I said only that the idea which I have of my soul does not represent it to me as dependent upon the body, and identified with it, that would be only an abstraction, from which I could only form a negative argument with a faulty conclusion. But I say that that idea represents it to me as a substance which can exist, even though everything which belongs to the body is excluded from it; from which I form a positive argument and conclude that it can exist without the body.

Letter to Mesland, May 2, 1644(?). IV, 120.

ACCIDENT

I certainly admit, to tell the truth, that one substance can be applied to another substance; but, when that happens, it is not the substance which takes the form of an accident, it is only the mode or the fashion in which it happens: for example, when clothing is applied to a man, it is not the clothing, but the being *clothed,* which is an accident.

Replies, VI. IX, 235.

❖ ❖ ❖

What we call an accident is anything that is present or absent whithout the corruption of the subject, although, when considered in itself, it might perhaps be a substance, as clothes are accidents of a man.

Letter to Regius, Dec., 1641. III, 460.

❖ ❖ ❖

It is not accidental that the human body is united to the soul, for that is its proper nature.

Letter to Regius, Dec., 1641. III, 460.

❖ ❖ ❖

See *substances*.

ACTION

Action and passion are one and the same thing, to which two different names have been given, by which it can be referred, at one time to the term from which the action starts,

2

and at another time to that at which it terminates, or in which it is received; so that there cannot be the least moment when there is a passion without an action.

Letter to "Hyperaspistas," Aug., 1641. III, 428.

❖   ❖   ❖

In corporeal things every action and passion consists in a single local motion, and it is called action when this motion is considered in the mover, and passion when it is considered in the thing which is moved; from which it also follows that, when these words are applied to immaterial things, it is necessary to consider something in them which is analogous to motion, and that that which is on the part of the mover must be called action, as is volition in the soul, and that which is on the part of the thing moved must be called passion, like intellection and vision in the same soul.

Letter to Regius, Dec., 1641. III, 454-455.

❖   ❖   ❖

See *passion*.

ACTION AT A DISTANCE
Often the motion of the smallest bodies extends its action to the greatest distances; and thus the light of the sun and the farthest stars passes in an instant to the earth.

Principles, III, 79. IX2, 147.

AEOLIPILES
What you see coming out of aeolipiles is similar to what you see in the vapors or smokes which come from water when it is placed next to the fire.

Letter to Mersenne, Feb. 25, 1630. I, 118.

AERIAL
Concerning the particles which I have called *aerial*, I do not include under this name all those which are separated from one another, but only those which, without being very agitated or very solid, move separately from one another; this makes the bodies where they are remain rarefied, and keeps them

from being readily condensed. And because the particles which compose the air are, for the most part, of this nature, I have called them *aerial*.

Description of Human Body, IV. XI, 260.

AFFECTIONS

See *emotions*.

AFFLICTIONS

All our afflictions, whatever they are, do not depend primarily on the reasons to which we attribute them, but only on the emotion and the internal turmoil that nature excites in us.

Letter to Pollot, Jan. 21, 1641. III, 279-280.

AGREEABLE

Among the objects of a sense, the most agreeable to the mind is not the one that is easiest to perceive with that sense, nor that which is hardest. It is the object of which the perception is not so easy that it overwhelms the natural inclination by which the senses tend toward their objects, nor so difficult that it fatigues the sense.

Compendium Musicae, II. X, 92.

AIR

After fire, there is nothing more liquid than air, and one can see with the naked eye that its particles move about individually.

The World, III. XI, 14.

❖　❖　❖

As for the second element, which can be taken as the element of Air, I conceive it as a very subtle liquid, in comparison with the third element; but, in comparison with the first, it has a certain size, and a certain shape, in each of its particles, and one must imagine that they are almost all round, and joined together, like grains of sand and dust.

The World, V. XI, 24-25.

❖　❖　❖

The air is nothing other than a mass of particles of the third element, which are so fine and so detached from one

4

another that they obey all the movements of the matter of the sky which is among them: which is the cause that the air is rare, liquid and transparent, and that the tiny particles of which it is composed can be of all sorts of shapes.

Principles, IV, 45. IX2, 226.

ALGEBRA

Now we see another type of arithmetic, called "algebra," which is destined to do for numbers what the ancients did for geometrical figures.

Rules, IV. X, 373.

AMERICA

One ought to place more faith in a single witness who, after making a voyage to America, tells us that he has seen the antipodes, than in a thousand others who have previously denied that there were any, without having any reason for it other than that they didn't know about them.

Replies, VI. IX, 227.

ANACLASTIC

Consider the case of a man who was a student of mathematics and who sought to find out about that line which in optics is called the "anaclastic": it is that in which parallel rays refract in such a matter that they all come together, after refraction, in a single point; our man will easily notice that the determination of that line depends on the ratio between the angles of refraction and the angles of incidence; but he will not be able to find out what that ratio is, inasmuch as it pertains not only to mathematics, but also to physics.

Rules, VIII. X, 393-394.

ANAGRAM

If we wanted to make the best anagram, by transposing the letters of some given word, it would not be necessary to go from the easiest to the most difficult, nor to distinguish the absolute from the relative, because this is not the place to do all that; it will suffice to examine the transpositions of the letters by means of an order such that the same combinations will never

5

appear twice, and that their number be divided into a certain number of classes, in such a way that the ones that we are searching for will be apparent when they appear.

Rules, VII. X, 391.

ANALYSIS

Analysis shows the true path by which a thing has been methodically invented, and shows how the effects depend upon their causes; in such a way that, if the reader wishes to follow, and look carefully at all that it contains, he will not understand whatever is demonstrated less perfectly, and make it less his own, than if he himself had invented it.

Replies, II. IX, 121.

❖   ❖   ❖

See *synthesis.*

ANALYTIC

The analytic manner of writing which I followed [in the *Meditations*] permits making suppositions sometimes, when one has not yet carefully examined the subject, as it appeared in my first Meditation, where I supposed many things which I then refuted in the following Meditations.

Replies, II. IX, 121.

ANGELS

We judge that the least of the angels are incomparably more perfect than men.

Letter to Chanut, June 6, 1647. V, 56.

❖   ❖   ❖

The knowledge of angels escapes us almost entirely, because, as I have said, we cannot derive it from our mind, and we also know nothing, which the subject ordinarily requires, about whether they can be united to a body, since the Old Testament often represents them in bodily form, and similar things. It is preferable for us to follow Scripture on this point and to believe that they were young men, that they appeared as such, and so on.

Burman. V, 157.

ANGER

Anger can sometimes excite a desire for vengeance so violent that it makes us imagine more pleasure in punishing our enemy than in saving our honor or our life.

Letter to Elisabeth, Sept. 1, 1645. IV, 285.

◈　◈　◈

In anger, a prompt desire for vengeance is often mixed with love, hate, and sadness.

Passions, II, 117. XI, 415.

◈　◈　◈

Anger is a species of hate or aversion, which we have against those who have done some evil, or who have attempted to do harm, not indifferently to anyone at all, but particularly to us.

Passions, III, 199. XI, 477.

◈　◈　◈

One can distinguish two species of anger: one is quite prompt, and has strong external manifestations, but nevertheless has little effect and can easily be appeased; the other does not appear so clearly at first, but eats away further at the heart and has more dangerous effects.

Passions, III, 201. XI, 479.

ANIMALS

All the movements of the lower animals are produced, even though they have absolutely no cognition of things, but only a purely bodily imagination.

Rules, XII. X, 415.

◈　◈　◈

As for animals, we certainly notice movements in them similar to those which follow our imaginations or sensations, but they do not for that reason have imaginations or sensations.

Letter to Gibieuf, Jan. 19, 1642. III, 479.

◈　◈　◈

See *beasts*.

ANIMATE BODY

If someone claims that a living being is an animate body, without having explained beforehand the sense of the words *body* and *animate*, and if he does not act otherwise as he goes through all the metaphysical degrees [of the tree of Porphyry], certainly he pronounces words, and even words which are arranged in a certain order, but he says nothing; for that does not signify anything which can be conceived and form a clear and distinct idea in our mind.

Search for Truth. X, 517.

ANTIPODES

In the discovery of the antipodes, the report of a few seamen who have gone around the earth was believed, rather than thousands of philosophers who did not believe that it was round.

Letter to Clerselier. IX, 212.

A POSTERIORI

As for what I supposed at the beginning of the *Meteorology*, I could not demonstrate it *a priori* without giving all my physics; but the experiments that I deduced necessarily from it, and which cannot be deduced in the same way from other principles, seemed to me to demonstrate it well enough *a posteriori*.

Letter to Vatier, Feb. 22, 1638. I, 563.

APPETITES

See *sensations*.

APPETITES, NATURAL

The first sense that I call internal comprises hunger, thirst, and all the other natural appetites; and it is excited in the soul by the movements of the nerves of the stomach, the throat. and all the other parts which serve natural functions, for which there are such appetites.

Principles, IV, 190. IX2, 311.

APPREHENSION

Apprehension [*receptio*] is an action or rather an animal passion similar to that of automata, by which we receive the motion of things.

Letter to Regius, May, 1641. III, 373.

A PRIORI

Those who can sufficiently examine the consequences of the [eternal] truths and of our rules will be able to know the effects by their causes; and, to explain myself in the terms of the School, will be able to have *a priori* demonstrations of everything that can be produced in the new World.

The World, VII. XI, 47.

ARGUMENTATION

In this life you do not see in God and by his light that he is one; but you conclude it from a proposition that you have made about him, and you derive it by the force of argumentation, which is a machine which is frequently defective.

Letter to Newcastle, Mar. or Apr., 1648. V, 139.

ARITHMETIC AND GEOMETRY

Of all the sciences known as yet, Arithmetic and Geometry alone are free from any taint of falsity or uncertainty.

Rules, II. X, 364.

❖ ❖ ❖

In the easiest sciences, arithmetic and geometry, we have sufficient evidence that the ancient Geometricians made use of a certain analysis which they extended to the resolution of all problems, though they begrudged the secret to posterity.

Rules, IV. X, 373.

❖ ❖ ❖

I would hope that the reader had a natural taste for the study of arithmetic and geometry, although I would prefer that he had never paid any attention to them, rather than having been taught in the ordinary way.

Rules, XIV. X, 442.

ARTERIES

The arteries are tubes, through which the blood, warmed and rarefied in the heart, passes from there into all the other parts of the body, to which it carries warmth and material for nourishing them.

Description of Human Body, I. XI, 227.

ARTS AND SCIENCES

Men erroneously compare the sciences, which entirely consist in the cognitive exercise of the mind, with the arts, which only the first appearance of the object which was presented, depend upon an exercise and disposition of the body.

Rules, I. X, 359.

ASPECTS

As for the sort of distinction that comes between two different aspects [*façons*] of the same substance, it is striking that we can know one of these aspects [or modes] without the other, as the shape without the motion, and the motion without the shape; but we cannot think distinctly about one or the other if we do not know that they both depend upon the same substance.

Principles, I, 61. IX2, 52.

ASTONISHMENT

The surprise [which produces wonder] has enough power to make the [animal] spirits, which are in the cavities of the brain, flow toward the spot where there is the impression of the object which is wondered at, so that sometimes all of them are impelled there, in such a way that they are all so occupied in conserving that impression that none of them flow into the muscles, nor even turn in any way from the first traces which they have followed in the brain: this makes the whole body remain immobile like a statue, and such that one can perceive nor, as a consequence, can one acquire any particular knowledge of it. It is that which is commonly called being astonished [or shocked]; and astonishment is an excess of wonder, which can never be anything but harmful.

Passions, II, 73. XI, 382-383.

ASTROLOGERS

All the astrologers, who know nothing about the nature of the heavenly bodies, and without ever having perfectly observed their movements, hope to be able to predict their influences.

Rules, V. X, 380.

ASTROLOGY

I see that those who brag about having secrets, for example in alchemy or in astrology, no matter how ignorant and impertinent they may be, never fail to find curious people who pay very well for their impostures.

Letter to Chanut, Mar. 31, 1649. V, 327.

ASTRONOMERS

With the aid of imaginary circles, astronomers describe their phenomena.

Rules, XII. X, 417.

ATHEISTS

Everything that the atheists say in combating against the existence of God always depends either on pretending that God has human affections, or on attributing to our minds so much force and wisdom that we have the presumption to want to determine and comprehend what God can and ought to do.

Meditations, Preface. VII, 9.

◈　◈　◈

As for the science of an atheist, it is easy to show that he cannot know anything with certainty and assurance; for, as I have already said, the less powerful he recognizes the author of his being to be, the more he will have occasion to suspect that his nature is so imperfect that he is deceived, even in the things that seem very evident to him; and he will never be able to escape from this doubt, if he does not first recognize that he has been created by a true God, principle of all truth, who cannot be a deceiver.

Replies, VI. IX, 230.

ATOMS

It implies a contradiction [to say] that there are atoms, or particles of matter which have extension and which nevertheless are indivisible, because one cannot have the idea of an extended thing, without being able also to have the idea of its half, or its third, or, as a consequence, without being able also to conceive it as divisible into two or three parts.

Letter to Gibieuf, Jan. 19, 1642. III, 477.

11

❖ ❖ ❖

There cannot be atoms, or particles of bodies which are indivisible, as some philosophers have imagined.

Principles, II, 20. IX2, 74.

❖ ❖ ❖

There is a contradiction in saying that there are atoms which are conceived as extended and at the same time indivisible, because, even though God could certainly have made them such that no creature could divide them, we cannot comprehend how he could deprive himself of the power to divide them himself.

Letter to More, Feb. 5, 1649. V, 273.

❖ ❖ ❖

See *particles.*

ATTRIBUTE

Whenever we see a quality assigned to anything by nature, whether it is a mode that can suffer change, or the very essence of that thing, manifestly unchangeable, we term that quality its attribute.

Notes against a Program, II. VIII 2, 348.

❖ ❖ ❖

All the attributes taken together are in truth the same thing as the substance, but not taken one by one, and separately from one another.

Burman. V, 155.

❖ ❖ ❖

ATTRIBUTE, PRINCIPAL

Each substance has a principal attribute; that of the soul is thought, and extension is that of the body.

Principles, I, 53. IX2, 48.

AUTOMATA

None of this will seem strange to those who, — knowing how many different *automata,* or moving machines, the industry of men can make, without using more than a very few pieces, in comparison with the great multitude of bones, muscles, nerves, arteries, veins, and all the other parts which are in the body of each animal, — consider the body as a machine, which, having been made by the hands of God, is incomparably better coordinated and has much more admirable movement in it, than any of those which could be invented by men.

Discourse, V. VI, 55-56.

❖   ❖   ❖

Never, unless it were by accident, would these automata respond, either by words or even by signs, appropriately to those who ask them questions.

Letter to Reneri, Apr. May, 1638. II, 40

❖   ❖   ❖

If we were accustomed to seeing automata which perfectly imitated all of our actions that they were able to imitate, and anything other than automata, because we would find they in any way that all animals which do not have reason were if we took them to be only automata, we would not suspect differ from us in all the same things as do the automata.

Letter to Mersenne, July 30, 1640. III, 121.

❖   ❖   ❖

See *machine*.

AVERSIONS

It is easy to think that the strange aversions of some people, such that they cannot bear the odor of roses, or the presence of a cat, or similar things, come only from the fact that at the beginning of their life they were badly injured by some similar objects, or they had some sensation in sympathy with an injury to their mother when she was pregnant.

Passions, II, 136. XI, 429.

AXIOMS

For all the time that they [axioms] are clearly and distinctly perceived [their truth is manifest], because our soul is of such a nature that it cannot refuse to accept whatever it comprehends distinctly; but because we often remember conclusions which we have derived from such premises, without paying attention to the premises themselves, I say then that without the knowledge of God we could claim that they are uncertain.

To Regius, May 24, 1640. III, 64.

❖ ❖ ❖

The knowledge of first principles or axioms is not usually called science by the dialecticians.

Replies, II. IX, 110.

❖ ❖ ❖

See *common notions; principles.*

B

BEASTS

He supposes that, according to me, the beasts see in the same way that we do, that is by sensing, or thinking that they see, the opinion that is believed to be that of Epicurus and which, even in our own time, is approved by nearly everyone.

Letter to Plempius, Oct. 3, 1637. I, 413.

⬦ ⬦ ⬦

The soul of beasts is nothing but their blood.

Letter to Plempius, Oct. 3, 1637. I, 414.

⬦ ⬦ ⬦

I have not only said that in beasts there were no thoughts, as some would have me believe, but in addition I have proved it with such strong reasons that I have not yet seen anyone who had anything worth considering in opposition to me.

Replies, VI. IX, 228.

⬦ ⬦ ⬦

I know very well that the beasts do many things better than we do, but that does not astonish me; because that even serves to prove that they act naturally, and by machinery, like a clock, which does a much better job of telling us what time it is than does our own judgment.

Letter to Newcastle, Nov. 23, 1646. IV, 575.

⬦ ⬦ ⬦

The greatest of all the prejudices which we have retained from our childhood is that of believing that the beasts think.

Letter to More, Feb. 5, 1649. V, 276.

⬦ ⬦ ⬦

See *animals; brutes.*

BEAUTIFUL

In general, neither the beautiful nor the agreeable signify anything other than a connection between our judgment and

15

the object; and because the judgments of men are so different, one cannot say that either the beautiful or the agreeable has any determinate measure.

Letter to Mersenne, Mar. 18, 1630. I, 133.

BEING BY ITSELF

We ought always to interpret the words *being by itself* [i.e., self-caused, substance] positively, and as if it were caused by a superabundance of its own power, which cannot be other than God's alone.

Replies, I. IX, 89.

❖   ❖   ❖

One can ask of every thing, if it is *by itself* or *by another;* and certainly by this means one can infer the existence of God, although one does not explain in formal and precise terms, how one ought to understand the words: *being by itself.*

Replies, IV. IX, 184.

❖   ❖   ❖

To be self-caused [as is God], means being by itself, and not having any other cause than its own essence, which could be called its formal cause.

Letter to °°°, Mar., 1642(?). V, 544.

❖   ❖   ❖

See *cause; substance.*

BELIEVE

The action of thought by which one believes a thing is different from that by which one knows that one believes.

Discourse, III. VI, 23.

BLACK

It [the color black] destroys the force of the rays which are reflected from the back of the eye toward the front, and prevents their returning from the back to the front again, where they could cause confusion.

Treatise on Man. XI, 155.

BLESSEDNESS

There is a difference among blessedness, the sovereign good, and the final end or goal toward which our actions ought to tend; for blessedness is not the sovereign good; but it presupposes it, and it is the contentment or satisfaction of the mind which comes from the fact that one possesses it. But, by the end of our actions, one can understand either one or the other; for the sovereign good is doubtless the thing which we ought to propose as the goal of all our actions, and the contentment of mind which comes from it is also properly called our end, since it is the attraction which makes us seek it.

Letter to Elisabeth, Aug. 18, 1645. IV, 275.

❖   ❖   ❖

Blessedness consists only in contentment of the mind, that is, in contentment in general.

Letter to Elisabeth, Aug. 18, 1645. IV, 277.

❖   ❖   ❖

See *happiness*.

BLOOD

The blood is nothing other than a mass of many tiny parcels of food which have been taken for nourishment.

Description of Human Body, III. XI, 250.

BLUSHING

One cannot easily keep oneself from blushing or turning pale, when some passion inclines toward it: because these changes do not depend upon the nerves and muscles, like the preceding [changes]; they come more immediately from the heart.

Passions, II, 114. XI, 413.

BODY

We do not form two ideas in our imagination, one of body, and the other of extension, but a single idea, that of an extended body.

Rules, XIV. X, 444.

❖   ❖   ❖

I suppose [in this Treatise] that the body is nothing other than a statue or machine made of earth, which God forms expressly.

Treatise on Man. XI, 120.

17

❖ ❖ ❖

I agree with those who say that man does not comprehend anything by means of the body and the argument by which you attempt to prove the contrary makes no impression on me; for although the body interferes with some of the functions of the soul, it can nevertheless be of no help to it for the knowledge of immaterial things, and can only hinder it on this occasion.

Letter to Regius, May, 1641. III, 374-375.

❖ ❖ ❖

Nature teaches me also by the sensations of pain, hunger, thirst, etc., that I am not only housed in my body, like a pilot in his ship, but, besides that, that I am conjoined very tightly and so mixed and mingled with it, that I compose a single whole with it.

Meditations, VI. IX, 64.

❖ ❖ ❖

The nature of body is such that none of its parts can be moved by another part at a distance from it, unless it can also be moved in the same way by each of the parts which are between the two.

Meditations, VI. IX, 69.

❖ ❖ ❖

I conceive fully what a body is (that is, I conceive body as a complete thing), when I think only that it is a thing, which is extended, shaped, mobile, etc., while I deny of it all the things which belong to the nature of mind.

Replies, I. IX, 95.

❖ ❖ ❖

The substance which is immediately the subject of extension and of the accidents which presuppose extension, like shape, position, local movement, etc., is called *Body.*

Replies, II. IX, 125.

❖ ❖ ❖

There are certain acts which we call *corporeal*, like size, shape, motion, and all the other things which cannot be con-

18

ceived without local extension, and we call by the name *body* the substance in which they reside.

Replies, III. IX, 137.

❖   ❖   ❖

Being extended, divisible, of a given shape, etc., are the forms or the attributes by means of which I know that substance which is called *body*.

Replies, IV. IX, 173.

❖   ❖   ❖

There is nothing which pertains to the nature or essence of body, except that it is a substance which is extended in length, breadth, and depth, capable of various shapes and motions; and its shapes and movements are nothing other than modes, which could not exist without it; but colors, odors, tastes, and other similar things are nothing but sensations which have no existence outside my thought, and which are no less different from bodies than pain is different from the shape or the motion of the arrow which causes it; and finally, weight, hardness, the ability to heat, to attract, to purge, and all the other qualities which we notice in bodies, consists solely in motion or in privation of motion, and in the configuration and arrangement of its parts.

Replies, VI. IX, 239.

❖   ❖   ❖

I find that the word body is quite equivocal; for, when we speak of a body in general, we understand a determinate part of matter, and altogether of the quantity of which the universe is composed, so that one could not take away ever so little from that quantity, without our judging immediately that the body is smaller, and that it is no longer whole, nor change any particle of that matter, without our thinking that the body is no longer totally the same, or numerically the same. But, when we speak of the body of a man, we do not understand a determinate part of matter, nor one which has a determinate size, but we merely understand all the matter which is, taken altogether, united with the soul of that man; in such a way that, even though that matter changes, and even though its

19

quantity increases or diminishes, we still believe that it is the same body, numerically the same, as long as it remains joined and substantially united to the same soul.

Letter to Mesland, Feb. 9, 1644. IV, 166.

❖　❖　❖

God has made our body as a machine and has willed that it function as a universal instrument; operating always in the same manner according to its own laws.

Burman. V, 163.

❖　❖　❖

The soul is truly joined to all the body, and it cannot be properly said to be in some one of these parts to the exclusion of the others, because the body is one, and in some fashion indivisible, because of the placement of its organs, which are all so related to one another that when one of them is taken away, that makes the whole body defective; and because the soul is of a nature which has no reference to extension, nor to dimensions, or other properties of the matter of which the body is composed, but simply to the whole union of its organs.

Passions, I, 30. XI, 351.

❖　❖　❖

See *corporeal substance; mind; matter.*

BOLDNESS

Boldness is a species of courage, which leads the soul to do the things that are the most dangerous.

Passions, III, 171. XI, 460.

BOOKS

For the greater number of books, one need only read a few lines and look at a few pictures, in order to know them entirely; the rest is there only to fill up the pages.

Cogitationes Privatae. X, 214.

❖　❖　❖

The books of the ancients are to be read, because there is an immense profit in being able to make use of the efforts of such a larger number of persons: not only in order to know what

20

has already been discovered in earlier times, but also in order to find out what problems still remain to be solved in each discipline.

Rules, III. X, 366.

❖   ❖   ❖

The reading of all good books is like a conversation with the best people of past centuries, who were the authors, and even a studied conversation, in which they show us only the best of their thoughts.

Discourse, I. VI, 5.

BRAIN

The opinion that [some people] have, that the particles of the brain concur with the mind in order to form our thoughts, is not founded upon any positive reason, but solely on the fact that they have never experienced being without a body, and that quite often they have been hindered by the body in their calculations; and it is the same as if someone who, from infancy, had irons on his feet judged that these irons were a part of his body, and were necessary for walking.

Replies, II. IX, 105.

BRUTES

As for the brutes, they never reach an age when anyone can notice the least sign of thought in them.

Letter to More, Apr. 15, 1649. V, 345.

C

CATHOLIC RELIGION

Since I am very zealous for the Catholic religion, I revere in general all its leaders. I do not add that I do not wish to run the risk of their censure; for, believing very firmly in the infallibility of the Church, and not doubting any of my reasonings either, I cannot fear that one truth is contrary to the other.

Letter to Mersenne, Dec., 1640. III, 259.

CAUSE

In order to show here that we are considering the purely cognitive interrelationships among things, and not the true nature of each, we have deliberately listed *cause* and *equality* among the "absolute" notions, even though their nature is actually relative: in fact, according to the philosophers, cause and effect are correlative terms; but in our perspective, if we seek to know which is the effect, it is necessary first to know the cause, and not conversely.

Rules, VI. X, 383.

❖   ❖   ❖

Now, it is a thing which is manifest by the natural light that there must be at least as much reality in the efficient and total cause as in its effect: for where would the effect be able to derive its reality, if not from its cause? and how would that cause be able to communicate the reality to the effect, if it did not have it in itself?

Meditations, III. IX, 32.

❖   ❖   ❖

The natural light does not tell us that it is necessary for the efficient cause to precede its effect in time.

Replies, I. IX, 86.

❖   ❖   ❖

The natural light tells us that there is nothing about which it is not permissible to ask why it exists, or of which one may

23

not search for the efficient cause, or, if it has no efficient cause, to ask why it has no need of one.

Replies, I. IX, 86.

❖   ❖   ❖

Everything which exists, exists either by a cause, or is as if it were its own cause.

Replies, I. IX, 89.

❖   ❖   ❖

It is a primary notion that there is nothing in an effect which has not been in a similar or more excellent way in the cause, which is so evident that there are no notions which are clearer; and that other common notion, that *from nothing nothing comes,* contains it in itself, because, if one says that there is something in the effect which has not been in the cause, he must also agree that that comes from nothing.

Replies, II. IX, 106.

❖   ❖   ❖

There is nothing which exists of which one cannot ask what the cause of its existence is.

Replies, II. IX, 127.

❖   ❖   ❖

All the reality or perfection which is in a thing is found formally, or eminently, in its first and total cause.

Replies, II. IX, 128.

❖   ❖   ❖

When it is a question of a universal and undeterminated cause, it seems to me that it is a very evident common notion that what is capable of the greater is likewise capable of the less, as well as that the whole is greater than its parts.

Letter to Mesland, May 2, 1644(?). Parts IV, 111.

CAUSE, TOTAL

The total cause [is] the cause of being itself; such a cause cannot produce anything which is not similar to itself, for, being itself being and substance, and producing something in giving being to it, that is, producing it out of nothing (a mode of production which belongs to God alone), that effect must at least be being and substance, and must thus be similar to God and represent his image.

Burman. V, 156.

CAUSED, SELF-

See *being by itself*.

CAUSES, FINAL

The whole class of [final] causes, which are customarily derived from their end [or purpose], is of no use in physics or natural [science]; for it does not seem to me that I can without excessive boldness search out and attempt to discover the impenetrable purposes of God.

Meditations, IV. IX, 44.

❖　❖　❖

We will not stop to examine the ends which God adopted in creating the world, and we reject entirely from our philosophy the search for final causes.

Principles, I, 28. IX2, 37.

❖　❖　❖

See *ends; purpose*.

CENSOR

I have almost never found a censor of my opinions who did not seem to me to be either less rigorous or less equitable than myself.

Discourse, VI. VI, 69.

CERTAIN KNOWLEDGE

There is no path to certain knowledge of the truth, other than evident intuition and necessary deduction.

Rules, XII. X, 425.

CERTAINTY

We should be concerned only with those objects of which our mind appears to be able to attain certain and indubitable knowledge.

Rules, II. X, 362.

◈ ◈ ◈

Whoever seeks the straight road to truth should not be concerned with any object about which he cannot obtain a certainty equal to that of the demonstrations of arithmetic and geometry.

Rules, II. X, 366.

◈ ◈ ◈

It is only concerning perfectly simple and absolute things that we can have certain knowledge.

Rules, VIII. X, 394.

◈ ◈ ◈

One might hope for as much certainty in matters which have to do with the conduct of life, as is required for the acquisition of science; but nevertheless it is very easy to demonstrate that one cannot seek or hope for so great a certainty.

Letter to "Hyperaspistas," Aug., 1641. III, 422.

◈ ◈ ◈

The certainty even of geometrical demonstrations depends upon the knowledge of God.

Meditations, Summary. IX, 11.

CERTAINTY, METAPHYSICAL

The other sort of certainty is when we think that it is not at all possible that the thing be other than we judge it to be. And it is founded upon a metaphysical principle which is most assured, which is that, since God is supremely good and the source of all truth, and since it is he that has created us, it is certain that the power of the faculty that he has given us for distinguishing the true from the false does not deceive, when we use it well, and when it shows us unmistakably that a thing is true.

Principles, IV, 206. IX2, 324.

CERTAINTY, MORAL

The first [type of certainty] is called moral, i.e., sufficient to determine our *mores* [customary behavior], or as great as that [which we have] concerning things which we do not customarily

26

doubt concerning the conduct of life, even though we know that it could happen, speaking absolutely, that they were false.

Principles, IV, 205. IX2, 323.

CHANCE

We cannot desire what we do not believe somehow to be possible, and we cannot believe that the things which do not depend upon us are possible, except insofar as we think that they depend upon chance, that is, that we judge that they can happen, and that similar thing have happened before. This opinion is founded only upon the fact that we do not know all the causes which contribute to each effect.

Passions, II, 145. XI, 438.

CHANGE

The continual change which is exhibited by the creatures is not inconsistent with the immutability of God, and seems even as an argument to prove it.

Principles, II, 42. IX2, 88.

CHARITY

Whatever sadness or pain that we have on such an occasion [sympathy for another], it is not as great as is the internal satisfaction which always accompanies our good works, and principally those which proceed from a pure affection for another which is wholly disinterested, that is, the Christian virtue which is called charity.

Letter to Elisabeth, Oct. 6, 1645. IV, 308-309.

CHIMERA

We can well imagine distinctly that a lion's head is grafted upon the body of a goat, without having to conclude that there is a chimera in the world: for reason does not tell us that what we see or imagine in this way is true.

Discourse, IV. VI, 40.

CHOLERIC HUMOR

The *choleric humor* is composed of promptness and disquiet, and malignity and confidence increase it.

Treatise on Man. XI, 167.

27

CHORD

It is one thing to say that a chord is sweeter than some other chord, and something else to say that it is more agreeable. For everyone knows that honey is sweeter than olives, and nevertheless many people will like to eat olives rather than honey.

Letter to Mersenne, Mar. 4, 1630. I, 126.

CIRCLE

No one ought to imagine that I am committing the fault that the logicians call a circle; for experience makes most of the effects very certain, and the causes from which I deduce then do not serve so much to prove them as to explain them.

Discourse, VI. VI, 76.

❖ ❖ ❖

You also say that *to prove effects by a cause, then prove that cause by the same effects, is a logical circle,* which I admit; but I do not admit that it is a circle when I explain the effects by a cause, then prove the cause by the effects: for there is a great difference between *proving* and *explaining.*

Letter to Morin, July 13, 1638. II, 197-198.

❖ ❖ ❖

It is not a circle to prove one cause by many effects which are known from elsewhere, then reciprocally to prove several other effects by that cause.

Letter to Morin, July 13, 1638. II, 198.

❖ ❖ ❖

I have not fallen into the error that is called a circle, because I have said that we are assured that the things that we conceive quite clearly and quite distinctly are all true only because God is or exists; and that we are assured that God is or exists only because we conceive it quite clearly and quite distinctly; while making the distinction between the things which we actually conceive quite clearly, and those which we remember having previously conceived quite clearly.

Replies, IV. IX, 189-190.

28

CLEAR

I call clear what is present and manifest to an attentive mind: just as we say that we see objects clearly when, being present, they act strongly enough, and when our eyes are disposed to look at them.

Principles, I, 45. IX2, 44.

See *distinct; obscure.*

CLOTHING

I wear the same clothing in the city as in the country; in the same way, I should not recommend my Almanac by the beauty of its cover.

Letter to Huygens, June, 1637.

CLOUDS

Although the clouds hardly exceed the summits of some mountains, and although they are sometimes even seen lower than the tips of our steeples, nevertheless, because one has to turn his eyes toward the sky to look at them, we imagine them so high that even the poets and the painters make the throne of God out of them, and make it appear that he uses his own hands to open and close the doors of the winds, to sprinkle the dew over the flowers, and to send the thunderbolt upon the cliffs.

Meteorology, I. VI, 231.

COLD

If cold is only a privation [of heat], then the idea of cold is not the cold itself insofar as it is objectively in the understanding, but something else which is falsely taken for that privation: namely it is a certain sensation which has no being outside the understanding.

Replies, IV. IX, 180-181.

COLOR

What makes us see light is nothing other than the fact that the matter of the second element, which I have said is composed of many tiny balls touching one another, is impelled [in various directions]; and that we can sense two motions of those balls, the one by which they come in a straight line toward our eyes, which gives us only the sensation of light; the other, by which they turn about their centers. In such a way that, if they turn much less quickly than they move in a straight line, the body from which they come appears *blue* to us, and if they turn much more rapidly, they appear *red* to us.

Description of Human Body, IV. XI, 255-256.

COLORS

If someone has been blind from birth, there is no hope that we could ever, by any argument whatever, make him conceive the true ideas of the colors, like those which we possess by means of our senses.

Rules, XIV. X, 438.

❖   ❖   ❖

You will perhaps even believe that colors are nothing else, in the bodies that are called colored, than the various ways in which those bodies receive [light] and retransmit it to our eyes.

Dioptrics, I. VI, 85.

❖   ❖   ❖

These colors [in afterimages] change as they grow weaker, which shows that their nature consists only in the different ways in which they move.

Dioptrics, VI. VI, 132.

❖   ❖   ❖

I have no taste for the philosophers' distinction, when they say that there are true [colors], and that others are only false or apparent. For, since all their true nature is nothing but appearing, it is, it seems to me, a contradiction to say that they are false and merely apparent.

Meteorology, III. VI, 335.

❖   ❖   ❖

When we say to someone that we perceive colors in objects, that it is the same as if we said to him that we perceived something in the objects about which we do not know the

30

nature, but which nevertheless causes a certain sensation in us, quite clear and manifest, which is called the sensation of colors.

Principles, I, 70. IX2, 57.

❖   ❖   ❖

COMETS

Those particles of matter which pass across various Skies ought to be taken to be Comets.

The World, IX. XI, 60-61.

❖   ❖   ❖

The principal things that are observed in [comets] are that they pass, one through one region of the sky, another through another, without following any rule that is known to us; and that we see one only during a few months, or sometimes even a few days; and that during this time they traverse never more, or rarely more, but often much less, than half of our sky.

Principles, III, 128. IX2, 179.

COMMON NOTIONS

The common notions are like chains joining other simple natures together, and upon the evidence of which lie all the conclusions which we attain by reasoning.

Rules, XII. X, 419.

❖   ❖   ❖

It is certainly a common notion to think that, if an intelligent nature is free, it is God.

Letter to Mersenne, Nov. 15, 1638. II, 435.

❖   ❖   ❖

I have denied only prejudices, and not the notions, like these, which are known without any affirmation or negation.

Letter to Clerselier. IX, 207.

❖   ❖   ❖

[Thought] encounters also various common notions, from which it composes demonstrations, which persuade it so absolutely that it cannot doubt their truth as long as it applies itself to them. For example, it has in itself the ideas of numbers and of shapes; it also has, among its common notions, "if one sets

31

quantities equal to other equal quantities, all will be equal
to one another," and many others which are as evident as this,
by which it is easy to demonstrate that the three angles of a
triangle are equal to two right angles, etc.

Principles, I, 13. IX2, 30.

❖   ❖   ❖

See *axioms; principles.*

COMPASSION

Those who are the most generous and who have the strongest
spirit, so that they do not fear any evil for themselves, and keep
above the power of fortune, are not exempt from compassion
when they see the infirmity of other men and understand their
complaints. For it is a part of generosity to have good will for
everyone.

Passions, III, 187. XI, 469-470.

COMPREHEND

To comprehend is to embrace the thought, but to know a
thing, it is enough to touch it with the thought.

To Mersenne, May 27, 1630? I, 152.

❖   ❖   ❖

Because the word *comprehend* signifies some limitation, a
finite mind could not comprehend God, who is infinite; but
that does not prevent its perceiving God, as one can certainly
touch a mountain, even though he cannot embrace it.

Letter to Clerselier. IX, 211.

CONDENSATION

When a body condenses, its pores shrink, in such a way that
some of the subtle matter which fills them is squeezed out, in
the same way that the water comes out of a sponge when it
is pressed.

Letter to Mersenne, Oct. 11, 1638. II, 384.

❖   ❖   ❖

When [we see that a body] is condensed, its particles are closer
together than they were, either because the intervals between

32

them are smaller, or because these intervals have been elimina-
ted altogether, in which case the body cannot conceivably be
condensed further.

Principles, II, 6. IX2, 66.

CONJECTURE

It is much easier to make some conjecture concerning a
subject chosen at random than it is to track down a single
subject, no matter how simple it is, until the truth is found.

Rules, II. X, 366.

❖   ❖   ❖

We engage in conjecture when, for example, from the fact
that water, which is farther from the center of the world than
is earth, is similarly of a lighter consistency; from the fact also
that air, which is above the water, is still less dense than water;
we conjecture that above the air there is nothing other than a
certain ether, which is very pure and much lighter than the
air itself, etc.

Rules, XII. X, 424.

CONSCIOUS

To be conscious is assuredly to think and to reflect upon ones
thought, but it is false that that cannot take place while the
preceding thought subsists, because, as we have already seen,
the soul can think many things at the same time, persevering in
its thought, and reflecting upon its thoughts whenever it wishes,
to be therefore conscious of its thought.

Burman. V, 149.

CONSERVATION

The natural light makes us see clearly that conservation and
creation differ only with regard to our way of thinking, and
not actually.

Meditations, III. IX, 39.

CONSIDERING

[Considering] is a special mode of thinking which takes place
as follows. When external objects act upon my senses, painting
their ideas or rather their shapes there, then the soul, when
it notices these images which are found painted upon the

33

[pineal] gland, is said to *sense*. When, on the contrary, these images are not painted upon the gland by the external objects themselves, but by the soul alone, which, in the absence of external things, represents them and forms them in the brain, then it is *imagination*; so that the difference between imagination and sensing consists solely in that in the second case, the images are painted by the soul, in the same way that, in the first case, they are painted by the external objects; one might say, in the second case, that they are painted with the windows closed.

Burman. V, 162.

CONTAINED

When we say that some attribute is contained in the nature or in the concept of a thing, it is the same as if we said that that attribute is true of that thing, and that one can be assured that it is in it.

Replies, II. IX, 125.

CONTEMPT

The passion of contempt is an inclination of the soul to consider the lowliness or smallness of that which it despises, caused by the movement of the [animal] spirits, which reinforce the idea of that smallness.

Passions, III, 149. XI, 444.

CONTROVERSY

In my writing I always want to follow the rule of never affirming anything about subjects which would ordinarily lead to controversy, without first giving the reasons which led me to those conclusions, and which seem to me to be able to persuade others.

Rules, XII. X, 411-412.

CORPOREAL

If by *corporeal* one understands everything that can, in any manner whatever, affect the body, the mind in this sense will also be said to be corporeal; but if by *corporeal* one understands what is composed of that substance which is called body, neither the mind nor even the accidents of the body ought to be called corporeal.

Letter to "Hyperaspistas," Aug., 1641. III, 424-425.

CORPOREAL SUBSTANCE

If it is said, for example, that a body is a corporeal substance, without at the same time defining what a corporeal substance is, these two words, *corporeal substance*, will not make us in any way more knowledgeable than the word *body*.

Search for Truth. X, 517.

❖ ❖ ❖

When [some people] distinguish [corporeal] substance from extension and size, either they understand nothing by the word substance, or they form in their mind only a confused idea of immaterial substance, which they falsely attribute to material substance, and attribute to extension the true idea of material substance, calling it an accident, so improperly that it is easy to see that their words have no connection with their thoughts.

Principles, II, 9. IX2, 68.

❖ ❖ ❖

See *body*.

COURAGE

When it is represented to us that [the outcome of a future event] depends upon us, there can be difficulty in the choice of the means or in the execution of it. From the first comes irresolution, which disposes us to deliberate and take counsel. To the last is opposed courage, or rashness, of which emulation is a species. And cowardice is contrary to courage, as fear or dread is to rashness.

Passions, II, 59. XI, 375-376.

❖ ❖ ❖

Courage, when it is a passion, and not a habit or natural inclination, is a certain warmth or agitation, which disposes the soul to try hard to do the things which it wants to do, of whatever nature they are.

Passions, III, 171. XI, 460.

35

COWARDICE

Cowardice is directly opposed to courage, and is a languor or coldness, which prevents the soul from carrying out the things that it would do if it did not have that passion.

Passions, III, 174. XI, 462.

CREATED THINGS

If God once withdrew his concurrence, all the things that he has created would return immediately to nothing, because before they were created, and before he gave his concurrence, they were only nothing.

Letter to "Hyperaspistas," Aug., 1641. III, 429.

CURIOSITY

So blind is the curiosity by which mortals are possessed that they often conduct their minds along unexplored routes, having no reason to hope for success, but merely being willing to risk the experiment of finding whether the truth they seek lies there. They are like someone who is burning with an unintelligent desire to find treasure, who continuously roams the streets, seeking to find something that a passerby might have chanced to drop.

Rules, IV. X, 371.

CUSTOMS

It is good to know something about the customs of various peoples, in order to judge our own more sanely.

Discourse, I. VI, 6.

❖　❖　❖

As for customs, it is necessary sometimes to follow opinions which are known to be quite uncertain, just as if they were indubitable.

Discourse, IV. VI, 31.

D

DEATH

Let us judge that the body of a living man differs as much from that of a dead man, as does a watch, or other automaton (that is, another machine which moves of itself), when it is wound up, and when it has within it the corporeal principle of the movements for which it is made, with everything that is required for its action, and the same watch, or other machine, when it is broken and when the principle of its movement has stopped.

Passions, I, 6. XI, 330-331.

DECEIVE

Although it seems that to be able to deceive is a mark of subtlety or of power, nevertheless the desire to deceive doubtless gives evidence of weakness or malice.

Meditations, IV. IX, 43.

DECEPTION

No deception into which men may fall (men, I say, not beasts) is due to faulty inference; it is caused merely by the fact that we admit certain badly understood experiences, or make judgments lightly, and without foundation.

Rules, II. X, 365.

◈   ◈   ◈

The understanding can never be deceived by any experience, provided only that it have a precise intuition of the object which is presented to it.

Rules, XII. X, 423.

◈   ◈   ◈

We can be deceived only when we ourselves make up, in some way or other, the things that we believe.

Rules, XII. X, 423.

The natural light teaches us that deception necessarily depends upon some fault.

Meditations, III. IX, 41.

❖   ❖   ❖

One can see clearly that it is impossible for God to be a deceiver, if one wishes to consider that the form or the essence of deception is a non-being, toward which the sovereign being can never incline.

Replies, VI. IX, 230.

DEDUCTION

By *deduction* we understand everything which is necessarily concluded from certain other things which are known with certainty. It was necessary to proceed thus, because most things which are known, with certainty are not evident in themselves; it suffices that they be deduced from true principles which are already known, by a continuous and uninterrupted movement of thought, which grasps each term with a clear intuition: in just the same way, we know that the last link of some long chain is attached to the first, even if we do not see all the intermediate links, upon which that attachment depends, with a single glance; it is enough that we have examined them one after the other, and that we recall that each of them, from the first to the last, is attached to its neighbors.

Rules, III. X, 369-370.

❖   ❖   ❖

The simple deduction of a single thing from some other thing is done by intuition.

Rules, XI. X, 407.

❖   ❖   ❖

Only by deduction can we compose things in such a way as to be certain of their truth.

Rules, XII. X, 424.

DELIGHT

Delight is particularly instituted by nature to represent the enjoyment of that which delights, as the greatest of all the

38

goods which belong to man: this makes one desire this enjoyment most ardently.

Passions, II, 90. XI, 395.

DEMONSTRATE

One can use the word *demonstrate* to mean both [*proving and explaining*], at least if it is taken according to common usage, and not in the particular signification that the philosophers have given it.

Letter to Morin, July 13, 1638. II, 198.

DEMONSTRATION

You ask whether I hold that what I have written about refraction is a demonstration; and I believe that it is, insofar as it is possible to give a demonstration of such a subject, without having previously demonstrated the principles of Physics by means of Metaphysics (which I hope to do some day, but which has not yet been done), and insofar as any other question of Mechanics, or of Optics, or of Astronomy, or any other subject which is not purely geometric, or arithmetic, has ever been demonstrated.

Letter to Mersenne, May 17, 1638. II, 141-142.

❖　❖　❖

There are two ways of demonstration: one is made by analysis or resolution, and the other by synthesis or composition.

Replies, II. IX, 121.

❖　❖　❖

See *mathematicians.*

DERISION

Derision or mockery is a species of joy mixed with hate, which comes from perceiving some small evil in a person who is thought to be worthy of derision.

Passions, III, 178. XI, 464.

DESIRES

Not every sort of desire is incompatible with blessedness; only those which are accompanied by impatience and sadness.

Letter to Elisabeth, Aug. 4, 1645. IV, 266.

39

Not only when one desires to acquire a good which one does not yet have, or to avoid an evil which one judges might happen, but also when one only hopes for the conservation of a good, or the absence of an evil: which is all that to which this passion extends: it is evident that it always has to do with the future.

Passions, II, 57. XI, 375.

❖   ❖   ❖

The passion of desire is an agitation of the soul, caused by the [animal] spirits, which disposes it to will for the future the things which it represents to itself as being suitable.

Passions, II, 86. XI, 392.

❖   ❖   ❖

Desire agitates the heart more violently than any of the other passions, and sends more [animal] spirits to the brain; these pass from there into the muscles, making all the senses more acute, and all the parts of the body more mobile.

Passions, II, 101. XI, 403.

❖   ❖   ❖

It seems to me that the error that is most often committed, concerning desires, is not to distinguish sufficiently between the things which depend entirely on us, and those which do not depend on us.

Passions, II, 144. XI, 436.

DESPAIR

When fear is so extreme that it takes away all place for hope, it is converted into despair; and this despair, representing the thing as impossible, extinguishes desire entirely, since desire is applied only to those things which are possible.

Passions, III, 166. XI, 457.

DEVOUT

When [self-satisfaction] is not justified, that is, when the actions from which one derives a great deal of satisfaction are not of great importance or even when they are vicious, it is ridiculous and serves only to produce an impertinent pride and arrogance. Which is particularly noticeable in those who, believing themselves to be devout, are only bigots and superstitious people, that is, who, under the cover of their frequent attendance at church, where they recite many prayers, wear short hair, fast, make contributions, think that they are entirely perfect, and imagine that they are such great friends of God that they could do nothing that would displease him, that everything that their passion suggests is a virtuous zeal: even though it sometimes suggests the greatest crimes which can be committed by men, like betraying cities, killing princes, exterminating entire peoples for the sole fact that they have not agreed with their opinions.

Passions, III, 190. XI, 471-472.

DIALECTIC

The rules by which dialectic attempts to direct the operations of the mind are useless here, and should even be regarded as obstacles, because nothing can be added to the pure light of reason which does not obscure it in some way.

Rules, IV. X, 372-373.

❖　❖　❖

[The study of dialectic] ruins good sense, rather than forming it, because insofar as it turns us away and leads us astray in these commonplaces and divisions which are external to the thing, it turns us away from the nature of the thing.

Burman. V, 175.

❖　❖　❖

See *logic*.

DIALECTICIANS

We omit all the rules of the dialecticians, by which human reason is said to be regulated.

Rules, X. X, 405.

DIFFERENCES, ESSENTIAL

I am busy conducting various experiments, to know the *essential differences* that there are between oils, spirits or cognacs, common waters and acids, salts, etc.

Letter to Mersenne, Apr. 5, 1632. I, 243.

DIMENSION

By *dimension* we understand nothing other than the method and the law by which any object is considered measurable.
Rules, XIV. X, 447.

DISAGREEMENT

Actually, in the sciences, it would be difficult to find a single question about which talented men do not often find themselves in disagreement.
Rules, II. X, 363.

DISDAIN

What I call disdain is the inclination of the soul to despise a free agent; it judges that, even though the nature of that agent is capable of doing good and evil, it is nevertheless so far below us that it cannot do either good or evil to us.
Passions, III, 163. XI, 455.

❖   ❖   ❖

See *veneration*.

DISGUST

And sometimes the duration of a good causes boredom or disgust; on the other hand, that of evil, a diminution of sadness.
Passions, II, 67. XI, 378.

❖   ❖   ❖

Disgust is a species of sadness, which comes from the same cause as that from which joy has previously come. For we are so composed that most things which we enjoy are lovely in our sight but for a time, and afterward become disagreeable.
Passions, III, 208. XI, 484.

DISPUTATIONS

I have never noticed that, by the method of disputations which is practiced in the schools, anyone has discovered any truth which was unknown previously; for, when each person attempts to win, he attempts to present the most plausible case, rather than weighing the reasons on one side and the other; and those who have been good lawyers for long are not likely, later, to be the best judges.
Discourse, VI. VI, 69.

DISTANCE

All the means which the soul will have to know the distance of the objects of sight are uncertain.

Treatise on Man. XI, 162.

❖   ❖   ❖

To understand what makes up the idea of the distance of objects, consider that, as the surface [of the pineal gland] changes its position, the points corresponding to places which are farther away from the center of the brain — these points are closer together, and conversely, the points corresponding to places which are closer to the brain are farther apart.

Treatise on Man. XI, 183.

DISTANCE VISION

Distance vision does not depend upon any images coming from objects, any more than does the perception of position, but, first, upon the shape of the body of the eye.

Dioptrics, VI. VI, 137.

❖   ❖   ❖

We know, in the second place, the distance of objects by the relationship of the two eyes to one another.

Dioptrics, VI. VI, 137.

❖   ❖   ❖

We have still another way of perceiving distance, namely the distinctness or confusion of the shape, and altogether by the force or weakness of the light.

Dioptrics, VI. VI, 138.

DISTINCT

It suffices for me to be able clearly and distinctly to conceive one thing without another, to be certain that the one is distinct or different from the other, because they can be posited separately, at least by the omnipotence of God.

Meditations, VI. IX, 62.

❖   ❖   ❖

[I call] distinct what is so precise and different from all other things that it contains only what appears manifestly to someone who considers it properly.

Principles, I, 45. IX2, 44.

See *clear*.

DISTINCTIONS

Learned men often make use of such subtle distinctions that they befog the light of nature, and find shadows in places where the unindoctrinated have no trouble.

Rules, XIV. X, 442.

DISTINCTIONS, MODAL

There are two sorts of modal distinctions, namely the distinction between the mode (which we have called the aspect), and the substance upon which it depends and which it distinguishes, and the other between two different modes (or aspects) of the same substance.

Principles, I, 61. IX2, 52.

DISTINCTIONS, REAL

[A formal distinction] suffices for conceiving one thing separately and distinctly from another, by an abstraction of the mind which conceives the thing imperfectly, but not for conceiving two things so distinct and separate from one another that we understand that each is a being which is complete and different from any other; since for that there is need of a real distinction.

Replies, I. IX, 94-95.

◆　　◆　　◆

There are distinctions of three kinds, namely, real, modal, and of reason, or rather what is made by thought. Real distinctions are properly found between two or more substances; for we can conclude that two substances are really distinct from one another from the sole fact that we can conceive one clearly and distinctly without thinking of the other.

Principles, I, 60. IX2, 51.

DIVISIBILITY

The extension of a body and its property of being divisible into many parts do not differ from the body which serves as the object, and vice versa [but the distinction is made], because we sometimes think confusedly of one without thinking of the other.

Principles, I, 62. IX2, 53.

DOCTORS

A man at the age of thirty years ought to have no need of a doctor, because at that age he can know well enough himself, by experience, what is useful or harmful to him, and thus be his own doctor.

Burman. V, 178.

DOG

If a dog has been whipped five or six times to the sound of a violin, then just as soon as he hears that music again, he will begin to whine and to run away.

Letter to Mersenne, Mar. 18, 1630. I, 134.

DOUBT

The person who doubts many things is no wiser than the man who has never thought about them.

Rules, II. X, 362.

❖   ❖   ❖

As for the doctor who says that we can doubt whether we are thinking or not, as well as we can doubt anything else, he shocks the natural light so violently that I am sure that no one, who thinks what he is saying, will share his opinion.

Letter to Mersenne, Apr. 21, 1641. III, 360.

❖   ❖   ❖

Of all the opinions which I had previously believed to be true, there is not one of them of which I cannot now doubt, not because of any lack of consideration or because of thoughtlessness, but for reasons which are very strong and maturely considered.

Meditations, I. IX, 17.

❖   ❖   ❖

From universal doubt, as from a fixed and unmovable point, I wish to derive the knowledge of God, of yourself, and finally of all the things which exist in nature.

Search for Truth. X, 515.

DREAMS

As for *dreams,* they depend in part upon the unequal force with which the [animal] spirits emerge from the [pineal] gland, and in part upon the impressions which are encountered in the memory: in such a way that they do not differ from the ideas which, as I have said before, are sometimes formed in the imagination of those who day-dream, except that the images which are formed during sleep can be much more distinct and vivid than those which are formed when one is awake.

Treatise on Man. XI, 197-198.

❖   ❖   ❖

When I considered that all the same thoughts that we have when we are awake can also come to us when we sleep, without any of them being true for all that, I resolved to pretend that all the things which had ever entered my mind were no more true than the illusions of my dreams.

Discourse, IV. VI, 32.

❖   ❖   ❖

How does one know that the thoughts which come in dreams are false, instead of the other way round, given that they are often just as vivid and precise?

Discourse, IV. VI, 38.

❖   ❖   ❖

At present I find a very notable difference [between sleeping and waking], in that our memory can never connect and join our dreams to one another and with the whole sequence of our life, as it usually joins together the things which happen to us when we are awake.

Meditations, VI. IX, 71.

❖   ❖   ❖

He who sleeps and dreams cannot perfectly and truthfully join and connect his dreams with the ideas of things past, even though he can think that he connect them. For who denies that a sleeper can be deceived? But afterward, when he is awake, he knows his error easily.

Replies, II. IX, 152.

The most philosophical person in the world could not prevent himself from having bad dreams, when his temperament inclined to them.

Letter to Elisabeth, Sept. 1, 1645. IV, 282.

DURATION

The duration of each thing is a mode or a way in which we consider that thing insofar as it continues to exist.

Principles, I, 55. IX2, 49.

❖   ❖   ❖

Because there is no substance which does not cease to exist when it ceases to endure, duration is not distinguished from substance except by thought.

Principles, I, 62. IX2, 53.

❖   ❖   ❖

I do not conceive the successive duration of things which are moved, or even that of their movement, in any way other than I conceive the duration of things which are not moved; for the before and after of all these durations, whatever they are, appear to me by the before and after of the successive duration which I discover in my thought, with which the other things are coexistent.

Letter to Arnauld, July 29, 1648. V, 223.

❖   ❖   ❖

I believe that it implies a contradiction to conceive of a duration between the [hypothetical] destruction of the first world and the creation of a new one; for if we connect that duration, or something similar, to the succession of the divine thoughts, that will be an error of the intellect, not a true perception of something.

Letter to More, Apr. 15, 1649. V, 343.

❖   ❖   ❖

See *time*.

E

EARTH

After the first two elements, I accept only one more, the third element; this is the element of Earth, of which I judge that the particles are so much larger and move as much more slowly, in comparison with those of the second element, as the second in comparison with the first.

The World, V. XI, 25.

❖   ❖   ❖

The earth, insofar as its light is concerned, is not different from the moon, Venus, Mercury, and the other planets.

Principles, III, 11. IX2, 107.

❖   ❖   ❖

The earth can be numbered among the planets, and the sun among the fixed stars.

Principles, III, 13. IX2, 108.

❖   ❖   ❖

Because we see that the earth is not sustained by columns, or suspended in the air by cables, but that it is surrounded on all sides by an extremely liquid sky, let us think that it is at rest, and that it has no propensity toward motion, given that we do not notice any motion in it; but let us not also believe that that can prevent it from being carried along by the current of the sky, and that it follows the sky's motion without being moved itself: just as a ship, which is not driven by the wind, or by oars, and which is not retained by anchors, remains at rest in the middle of the sea, even though the tides of that great mass of water carry it insensibly along with it.

Principles, III, 26. IX2, 113.

❖   ❖   ❖

If hereafter, to accommodate ourselves to general usage, we seem to attribute some movement to the earth, it must be thought that this is an improper manner of speaking.

Principles, III, 29. IX2, 115.

❖　❖　❖

Because there is no void around the earth, and because it does not itself have the force which makes it turn in twenty-four hours upon its axis, but is carried by the current of the matter of the sky which surrounds it and which penetrates everywhere into its pores, the earth ought to be considered as a body which has no motion.

Principles, IV, 22. IX2, 211.

❖　❖　❖

That we conceive our sky and our earth as so great, as though they contained everything — that comes from our prejudices: we consider the earth as the end of all and we do not think that it is a planet, like the others, which moves as do Mars, Saturn, etc., which we do not value nearly so highly.

Burman. V, 171.

EARTH, MOTION OF

Galileo's proofs of the motion of the earth are very good; but it seems to me that he does not present them in such a way as to persuade; for the digressions that he mixes in among them make one forget the first ones by the time one reads the last ones.

Letter to Mersenne, Aug. 14, 1634. I, 305.

❖　❖　❖

I could not separate [my philosophy] from [the doctrine of] the motion of the earth, because all my physics depends upon it.

Letter to Mersenne, Dec., 1640. III, 258.

EASY

Most thinking people despise it when you make things too easy for them.

The World, VII. XI, 48.

ECHOS

The objection which was made against your experiments concerning echos does not seem to me to be of any importance: for even though it is true that the sound extends in circles on all sides, like the movement which occurs in water when a stone is thrown in it, it is necessary in any case to notice that the circles extend much farther on the side toward which the stone is thrown, or toward which one is turned when speaking, than toward the other side; from which it follows that the echo, which is only the result of the reflection of the part of the circles which go farthest, only extends toward the side from which it is reflected.

Letter to Mersenne, Jan. 25, 1638(?). I, 503-504.

EFFORT

See *inclination*.

ELEMENTS

There is only one material substance, which receives the action or the means for its local motion from an external agent, from which it derives various figures or modes, which make it such as we see it, in its primary composite forms, which are called *elements*. You have noticed, moreover, that the nature of these elements or primary composites, called Earth, Water, Air and Fire, consists only in the difference between the fragments or small and large particles of that matter, which continually change from one to the other, by heat and movement, from gross to subtle; or into "innobles," that is, from subtle to gross, when the action of heat and movement begins to diminish. From the first mixing of these four primary elements there results a mixture which could be called the fifth element.

Letter to Villebressieu, Summer, 1631. I, 216.

❖ ❖ ❖

I do not accept any elements other than the three that I have just described.

The World, V. XI, 26.

❖ ❖ ❖

All the bodies of this visible world are composed of these three forms in which matter is found, as though they were three different elements: namely that the sun and the fixed stars have the form of the first of these elements; the skies, that of the second; and the earth, with the planets and the comets, that of the third.

Principles, III, 52. IX2, 129.

51

It seems to me that I am probably correct in making use of these three characteristics, to be luminous, to be transparent, and to be opaque or obscure, which are the principal characteristics which can be related to the sense of sight, for distinguishing the three elements of this visible world.

Principles, III, 52. IX2, 129.

❖ ❖ ❖

See *air; earth; fire; magnet.*

EMINENTLY

See *formally.*

EMOTIONS

[The passions] could best be called emotions of the soul, not only because that name can be attributed to all the changes which happen in the soul, that is, to all the various thoughts which come to it, but particularly because, of all the sorts of thoughts that it can have, there are no others which agitate it and shake it so strongly as the passions.

Passions, I, 28. XI, 350.

❖ ❖ ❖

See *sensations.*

EMOTIONS, INTERNAL

Our good and our bad depend principally upon internal emotions, which are not aroused in the soul except by the soul itself; in which they differ from the passions, which always depend upon some motion of the [animal] spirits.

Passions, II, 147. XI, 440.

EMULATION

[Emulation] is nothing other than a warmth, which disposes the soul to undertake things at which it hopes to be able to succeed, because it has seen others succeed.

Passions, III, 172. XI, 461.

ENDS

It is something which is manifest in itself, that we cannot know the ends of God, if he himself does not reveal them to us.

Letter to "Hyperaspistas," Aug., 1641. III, 431.

It would be an absurd and puerile thing to claim in metaphysics that God, in the manner of a vain man, had no other end in constructing the world than being praised by men, and that he had created the sun, which is many times greater than the earth, with no other design than to give light to man, who occupies only a very tiny part of the world.

Letter to "Hyperaspistas," Aug., 1641. III, 431-432.

◈   ◈   ◈

See *causes, final.*

ENEMIES

I even include, under the name enemies, all those who are neither friends nor allies, because one has the right to make war upon them, when one finds it to his advantage.

Letter to Elisabeth, Sept., 1646. IV, 488.

ENUMERATION

To complete our science, we must review, as a whole and one by one, with a continuous and absolutely uninterrupted movement of thought, everything which concerns our subject, and include them in a sufficient and ordered enumeration.

Rules, VII. X, 387.

◈   ◈   ◈

This enumeration or [mathematical] induction is thus a review or inventory of all those matters that have a bearing on the problem raised, which is so thorough and accurate that by its means we can clearly and with confidence conclude that we have omitted nothing by mistake.

Rules, VII. X, 388.

◈   ◈   ◈

We should note that by sufficient enumeration or [mathematical] induction, we understand only that by which one arrives at a truth with greater certitude than by any other type of proof, with the exception of simple intuition.

Rules, VII. X, 389.

❖ ❖ ❖

We have defined enumeration as an inference based upon a large number of diversified propositions.

Rules, XI. X, 407.

❖ ❖ ❖

See *induction, mathematical.*

ENVY

What is commonly called envy is a vice which consists in a perversity of nature which makes certain people vexed over the good which they see happen to other men. But I use the word here to signify a passion which is not always vicious. Envy, therefore, insofar as it is a passion, is a species of sadness mixed with hate, which comes from seeing good happen to those who are not thought to be worthy of it.

Passions, III, 182. XI, 466.

EQUALITY

Equal things correspond to one another reciprocally; but we recognize those which are unequal only by comparing them to equal things, and not conversely, etc.

Rules, VI. X, 383.

❖ ❖ ❖

Because there is no proportion, nor any order, which is simpler to understand than that which consists in a perfect equality, I have supposed here that all the particles of matter were, in the beginning, equal among themselves, both in size and in motion, and I have not wanted to conceive any other inequality in the universe, except that which is in the position of the fixed stars, which appears so clearly to anyone who looks at the sky during the night, that it cannot be doubted.

Principles, III, 47. IX2, 126.

ERROR

Error can exist only concerning composite objects which the understanding itself fabricates.

Rules, VIII. X, 399.

In all these things we are subject to error: when someone tells us a fable, and we believe that it is a true story; when also a man who suffers from jaundice believes that everything is yellow, because he has a yellow color in his eyes; finally, when, due to the effect of an illness of the imagination (as with melancholics), we believe that the disordered images which are formed there represent true realities.

Rules, XII. X, 423.

❖   ❖   ❖

It is in our power to avoid an error if we are on our guard always to establish a connection between two things such that we see by intuition that the connection of one with the other is absolutely necessary.

Rules, XII. X, 424-425.

❖   ❖   ❖

The human mind generally falls into two sorts of error, when it supposes more than it has been given for the determination of the question, and when it neglects something that has been given.

Rules, XIII. X, 435.

❖   ❖   ❖

Error can only exist in the understanding, which I suppose, nevertheless, to remain free and to consider as doubtful that which is doubtful.

Letter to Reneri, Apr.-May, 1638. II, 35

❖   ❖   ❖

The error which is born [of precipitate judgment] is a privation with respect to ourselves, and a pure negation with respect to God.

Letter to Regius, May 24, 1640. III, 65

❖   ❖   ❖

I know that error, insofar as it is error, is not something real which depends upon God, but is simply a lack.

Meditations, IV. I, 43.

❖　❖　❖

Error is not a pure negation, i.e., is not the simple lack or absence of some perfection to which I am not entitled, but rather is a privation of some knowledge which it seems that I ought to possess.

Meditations, IV. IX, 43-44.

❖　❖　❖

I find that they [my errors] depend upon the concurrence of two causes, namely, the power of knowing which is in me, and the power of choosing, or rather my free will; i.e., my understanding and with it my will.

Meditations, IV. IX, 45.

❖　❖　❖

I think that all the errors that happen in the sciences come from our having judged too hastily in the beginning, admitting as principles things which were obscure and of which we did not have any clear and distinct notion.

Search for Truth. X, 526.

❖　❖　❖

Because it often happens that we make mistakes, even though God is not a deceiver, if we wish to search out the cause of our errors and discover their source, in order to correct them, we must take note that they do not depend upon our understanding so much as upon our will, and that they are not things or substances which require the actual concurrence of God to be produced: such that they are not, from his point of view, anything other than negations, that is, that he has not given us all that he could give us, and that we see by the same means that he was not required to give it to us; even though, from our point of view they are faults and imperfections.

Principles, I, 31. IX2, 38-39.

❖　❖　❖

See *Falsehood.*

ESSENCE

I think that it is necessary to show that between *the efficient cause,* properly so called, and *no cause,* there is something which holds to the mean, as it were, namely, *the positive essence of a thing.*

Replies, IV. IX, 185.

❖   ❖   ❖

A distinction must be drawn between things which from their nature can change, like the fact that I am at present either writing or not writing, that one man is prudent, another imprudent; and things which never change, such as are all the things that pertain to the essence of anything, as is generally acknowledged by philosophers.

Notes against a Program, II. VIII 2, 347.

❖   ❖   ❖

Everything that can be clearly and distinctly conceived in a chimera is a true being, and not fictitious, because it has a true and immutable essence, and that essence comes from God just as does the actual essence of other things.

Burman. V, 160.

❖   ❖   ❖

See *natures, true and immutable*.

ESTEEM

To wonder is joined esteem or scorn, according to whether it is the greatness or the smallness of an object that excites our wonder.

Passions, II, 54. XI, 373.

❖   ❖   ❖

Esteem, insofar as it is a passion, is an inclination of the soul, to represent to itself the value of the thing esteemed, which inclination is caused by a particular movement of the [animal] spirits, flowing in such a way in the brain, that they fortify the impressions there which pertain to this subject.

Passions, III, 149. XI, 443-444.

ETERNITY

The time that we live in this world is so little a thing in comparison with eternity that we ought not to care much whether we are taken too soon or too late.

To Colvius, June 14, 1637.

❖   ❖   ❖

[Eternity] is all together and all at once if you understand that nothing can be added and nothing taken away from the nature of God. But it is not all together and all at once if you understand that it exists all at the same time.

Burman. V, 148-149.

ETHICS

One of the points of my ethics is to love life without fearing death.

Letter to Mersenne, Jan. 9, 1639. II, 480.

EVIL

See *good*.

EVILS

There is a very great difference between the things which are made by the positive action of God, which could not be other than very good, and those which happen because of the cessation of that positive action, like all the evils and sins, and the destruction of a being, if any existent being were ever destroyed.

Letter to "Hyperaspistas," Aug., 1641. III, 429-430.

EXCESS

There are two sorts of excess: one which, changing the nature of the thing, and from good, making it bad, prevents its being submitted to reason; the other simply augments the measure, and only makes the good thing better.

Letter to Elisabeth, Nov. 3, 1645. IV, 331-332.

EXHALATIONS

See *vapors*.

EXISTENCE

Each person can see by intuition that he exists and that he thinks.

Rules, III. X, 368.

❖   ❖   ❖

I exist; therefore, God exists.

Rules, XII. X, 421.

It is necessary to make a distinction between possible existence and necessary existence; and to notice that possible existence is contained in the concept or the idea of all the things which we conceive clearly and distinctly, but that necessary existence is contained only in the idea of God.

Replies, I. IX, 92.

✧   ✧   ✧

In the idea or the concept of each thing, existence is contained, because we cannot conceive anything except under the form of a thing which exists; but with the difference that, in the concept of a limited thing, possible or contingent existence alone is contained and in the concept of a supremely perfect being, perfect and necessary existence is comprised.

Replies, II. IX, 128.

✧   ✧   ✧

It is necessary only to know what is meant by the word [existence]; one knows it immediately as completely as it is possible for man to know it, and for this there is no need of definitions; they obscure the thing rather than clarifying it.

Search for Truth. X, 525.

✧   ✧   ✧

We can conceive essence without actual existence, as the rose in winter; but they cannot be separated in reality, as they are usually distinguished, because the essence has not been before the existence, which is nothing other than the essence existing, so that the one is not prior to the other, and it is neither different nor distinct.

Burman. V, 164.

EXISTENCE, NECESSARY

Necessary existence is contained in the idea of a supremely powerful being, not by any fiction of the understanding, but because it belongs to the true and immutable nature of such a being to exist.

Replies, I. IX, 94.

The idea of an all-perfect Being is not in [thought] as a fiction, as is that which represents a chimera, but on the contrary, it is imprinted there by an immutable and true nature, and which must necessarily exist, because it cannot be conceived except with a necessary existence.

Principles, I, 15. IX2, 31.

EXPERIENCE

Philosophers who neglect experience seem to think that truth will be born out of their heads, like Minerva out of the head of Jupiter.

Rules, V. X, 380.

EXPERIMENTS

It is almost impossible to reason well concerning the experiments which others have done, because each person looks at things from a bias which is particular to himself.

Letter to Mersenne, Jan. 9, 1639. II, 489.

◈ ◈ ◈

Even experiments often give us occasion for being deceived, when we do not pay enough attention to all the causes that they can have.

Description of Human Body, II. XI, 242.

EXTENSION

By *extension* we understand everything which possesses length, breadth, and depth.

Rules, XIV. X, 442.

◈ ◈ ◈

By *extension* we do not mean anything which is distinct and separate from the subject itself.

Rules, XIV. X, 442.

◈ ◈ ◈

I do not conceive any extended substance in God, the angels, or in our soul; but only some thing extended in potency or an extension in potency; so that an angel could proportion this power of extension, sometimes to a larger and sometimes to a smaller part of corporeal substance.

Letter to More, Apr. 15, 1649. V, 342.

EXTERNAL OBJECTS

Since I am assured that I cannot have any knowledge of external objects except by the intermediary of the ideas of them which I have in myself, I am very careful not to report my immediate judgments [as though they were] about objects, nor to attribute anything positive to them other than what I previously perceived in their ideas; but I also believe that everything which is found in these ideas is necessarily in the objects.

Letter to Gibieuf, Jan. 19, 1642. III, 474.

F

FACULTIES

Looking within ourselves, we notice that the understanding, by itself, is capable of knowledge; but, in addition, three other faculties can give it help or impede it: the imagination, the senses, and the memory.

Rules, VIII. X, 398.

◈ ◈ ◈

The two principal faculties of the mind are perspicacity, intuiting single things distinctly, and sagacity, skillfully deducing one thing from another.

Rules, IX, X, 400.

◈ ◈ ◈

In us, there exist only four faculties which we can use to obtain knowledge: the understanding, the imagination, the senses, and the memory.

Rules, XII. X, 411.

FACULTY

God does not have the faculty of depriving himself of his own existence. For, by "faculty," we usually designate some perfection. But it would be an imperfection in God to be able to deprive himself of existence.

Letter to °°°, Mar., 1642(?). V, 544.

◈ ◈ ◈

Existence in any faculty is not actual but merely potential existence, since the very word *faculty* designates nothing more or less than a potentiality.

Notes against a Program, XIV. VIII 2, 361.

FAINTING

Fainting is not far removed from death. For one dies when the fire which is in the heart goes out completely; and one

63

falls only into a faint when it is smothered in such a way that it still retains some of its heat, which can later rekindle it.

Passions, II, 122. XI, 418.

FAITH

The truths of faith have always been the first in my belief.

Discourse, III. VI, 28.

❖   ❖   ❖

Although it is said that faith has obscure things as objects, nevertheless our reason for believing them is not obscure, but clearer than any natural light.

Replies, II. IX, 115.

FALL

The distance through which heavy bodies pass, when they fall, is proportional to the square of the time that they require for falling.

Letter to Mersenne, Aug. 14, 1634. I, 304.

FALSE

If they [ideas] are false, i.e., if they represent things which do not exist, the natural light makes me know that they proceed from nothing.

Meditations, III. IX, 35.

FALSEHOOD

If we frequently have [ideas] which contain falsehood, that can be only because they have something confused and obscure, insofar as they participate in nothingness, that is, they are so confused in us only because we are not completely perfect.

Discourse, IV. VI, 38.

FALSE OPINION

If some people are still persuaded to hold such a false opinion [as that ideas are like their objects], it is only because they give so much weight to judgments that they have made since the time that they were infants, and because they cannot forget them, and make other more solid judgments.

Principles, I, 67. IX2, 56.

FAT

Fat does not grow in the body like flesh, by nourishment properly so-called, but only because many of its particles join together, accumulating one upon another, as do non-living things.

Description of Human Body, III. XI, 249.

FAVOR

The good which has been done by others is cause for us to show favor to them, even when it was not to us that they did it; and if it is to us, we join gratitude to favor.

Passions, II, 64. XI, 377-378.

❖   ❖   ❖

Favor is properly a desire to see good happen to someone, for whom one has good will; but I use the word here to signify that will, insofar as it is excited in us by some good act of the person for whom we have it.

Passions, III, 192. XI, 473.

FEAR

Fear is another disposition of the soul, which persuades the soul that [what it desires] will not happen.

Passions, III, 165. XI, 456.

❖   ❖   ❖

Fear or terror, which is contrary to boldness, is not only a coldness, but also a confusion and astonishment of the soul, which takes away its power to resist the evils which it thinks are imminent.

Passions, III, 174. XI, 462.

FINITE

It repels my thought, or, what is the same, thing, it implies a contradiction [to say] that the world is finite or bounded, because I cannot avoid conceiving a space beyond the limits of the world, wherever I place these limits; but such a space is, according to me, a true body.

Letter to More, Apr. 15, 1649. V, 345.

FIRE

I conceive the first element, which can be called the element of Fire, as a liquid, the most subtle and penetrating thing in the world.

The World, V. XI, 24.

◈   ◈   ◈

Any violent motion suffices to produce fire.

Principles, IV, 87. IX2, 247.

FIRES WITHOUT LIGHT

In [man's] heart there is one of the fires without light, which I had already explained, and which I conceived as being of the nature of that which heats the hay, when it has been stored before it is dry, or which makes new wines boil, when they are fermented with the skins and pulp.

Discourse, V. VI, 46.

FIRMAMENT

Since the locations at which the stars are seen remain firm, and have not appeared to change since the astronomers first noted them, it seems to me that the firmament is nothing other than the surface which separates one vortex from another, and which cannot be changed, since the apparent locations of the stars do not change.

Principles, III, 131. IX2, 182.

FIRST NOTIONS

After reflection, we easily abandon all the prejudices which are founded only upon our senses, and we make use only of our understanding, because in the understanding alone the first notions or ideas, which are like the seeds of the truths that we are capable of knowing, are found naturally.

Principles, II, 3. IX2, 65.

FLAME

The body of the flame which acts upon the wood is composed of small particles which move separately from one another, with a very prompt and violent movement.

The World, II. XI, 8.

FLINT

I believe that the cause of fire, thus produced [i.e., with flint and steel], consists in the fact that the flints are hard and stiff (i.e., such that, if some of their particles are bent ever so slightly, they tend to return to their first shape, just as does a bow which is bent), and, in addition, are brittle.

Principles, IV, 84. IX2, 245.

FLUIDS

There is no other difference between those [parts of the body] which are called *fluids,* like blood, humors, spirits, and those which are called *solids*, like bones, flesh, nerves and membranes; except that each particle of the latter moves much more slowly than those of the former.

Description of Human Body, III. XI, 247.

FOLLOWERS

They [followers of Aristotle] are like the ivy, which does not tend to climb higher than the trees which hold it up.

Discourse, VI. VI, 70.

FORCE

It is certain, from the fact alone that a body has begun to move, that it has in itself the force to continue to move; just as, from the fact alone that it is stopped in some place, it has the force to continue to remain there.

Letter to Mersenne, Oct. 28, 1640. III, 213.

FORMALLY

The same things are said to be *formally* in the object of ideas, when they are in them such as we conceive them; and they are said to be there *eminently* when they are not truly in the ideas as we conceive them, but when they are so great that they can overcome this lack by their excellence.

Replies, II. IX, 125.

❖   ❖   ❖

Since the ideas themselves are [here taken as] nothing but forms, and since they are not composed of matter, always and every time that they are considered insofar as they represent

67

some thing, they are not taken *materially* but *formally;* but if they are considered, not insofar as they represent one thing or another, but solely as being operations of the understanding, one could well say truly that they are taken materially, but then they would not be concerned with the truth or the falsity of their objects.

Replies, IV. IX, 180.

FORMS, SUBSTANTIAL

We can very well conceive how the movement of a body can be caused by that of another, and varied by the size, shape, and position of its parts, but we cannot understand in any way how these same things, namely, size, shape, and motion, could produce natures which are entirely different from theirs, such as are those of real qualities and substantial forms, which the majority of philosophers have supposed to be in bodies; neither can we conceive how these forms or qualities, being in the bodies, could have the force to move other bodies.

Principles, IV, 198. IX2, 317.

FREE

It is manifest by the natural light that there could be only one sovereign being who is free of any other.

Letter to "Hyperaspistas," Aug., 1641. III, 428.

❖　❖　❖

In order to be free, it is not necessary that I be indifferent to the choice between one or the other of two contraries; but rather, all the more that I lean toward the one, given either that I know with certainty that the good and the true are found there, or that God disposes my internal thought in this direction, all the more freely do I make the choice of it and adopt it.

Meditations, IV. IX, 46.

❖　❖　❖

I generally call free, everything which is voluntary.

Letter to Mesland, May 2, 1644(?). IV, 116.

God was as free to make it untrue that all the lines drawn from the center of a circle to its circumference are equal, as to leave the world uncreated.

Letter to Mersenne, May 27, 1630. I, 152.

❖　❖　❖

All that we conceive as distinctly possible, is possible; and we conceive distinctly that it is possible that the world has been produced; therefore it has been produced: this is a chain of reasoning that I entirely approve. And it is certain that one could not conceive distinctly that the sun or any other finite thing is free; for freedom, when it is conceived distinctly, includes infinity.

Letter to Mersenne, Sept. 30, 1640.

❖　❖　❖

Although perhaps there are many who, when they consider the preordination of God, cannot comprehend how our freedom can exist and be consistent with his, still there is no one who, looking only at himself, does not sense and experience the fact that will and freedom are the same thing, or rather that there is no difference between what is voluntary and what is free.

Replies, III. IX, 148.

❖　❖　❖

We experience within ourselves a freedom which is such that, whenever we wish, we can abstain from believing the things which we do not know well, and thus keep ourselves from ever being deceived.

Principles, I, 6. IX2, 27.

❖　❖　❖

A greater freedom actually consists either in a greater facility for self-determination, or in a greater use of that positive power that we have to follow the worse, even while we see the better.

Letter to Mesland, Feb. 9, 1645. IV, 174.

❖　❖　❖

See *Indifference*.

FREE WILL

The extreme perfection that we notice in certain actions of the animals makes us suspect that they do not possess free will.

Cogitationes Privatae. X, 219.

❖ ❖ ❖

You are correct in saying that we are as assured of our free will as of any other first notion; for it is truly one of them.

Letter to Mersenne, Dec., 1640. III, 259.

❖ ❖ ❖

It is so evident that we have a free will, which can give its consent or not give it, when it seems good to it, that this can be counted as one of our most common notions.

Principles, I, 39. IX2, 41.

❖ ❖ ❖

It is always possible for us to refrain from following a good which we know clearly, or from admitting an evident truth, provided that we think that it is a good to affirm our free will by such an act.

Letter to Mesland, Feb. 9, 1645. IV, 173.

❖ ❖ ❖

The greatest and most solid contentment of life comes from the proper use of the free will.

Letter to Christine, Nov. 20, 1647. V, 84.

G

GAIETY

What I call gaiety is a species of joy, in which there is the peculiar quality that its sweetness is augmented by the memory of evils which one has suffered, and from which one feels himself relieved, in the same way that he would if he felt himself discharged of some heavy burden, which he had carried for a long time upon his shoulders.

Passions, III, 210. XI, 485.

GAY

It is better to be less gay and have more knowledge.

Letter to Elisabeth, Oct. 6, 1645. IV, 305.

GENERATION

Simple alteration is that which does not change the form of the subject, as when wood becomes warmer, and generation is that which changes the form, as when wood is consumed by fire.

Letter to Regius, Dec., 1641. III, 461.

❖   ❖   ❖

Generation is to be considered in two ways, one without semen or womb, the other from semen.

Generatio Animalium. XI, 505.

GENEROSITY

I believe that the true generosity, which gives a man the highest self-esteem that he can legitimately have, only consists, partly in that he knows that there is nothing which truly belongs to him other than the free determination of his acts of will, nor reason to be praised or blamed, except because he uses it well or badly; and partly in that he senses in himself a firm and constant resolution to use it well, that is, never to

71

lack the will to undertake and execute all the things which he judges to be the best. Which is to follow perfectly the course of virtue.

Passions, III, 153. XI, 445-446.

GENESIS

Whoever explains [the book of Genesis to me], or the Song of Solomon or the book of Revelation, would seem to me to be a veritable Apollo.

Burman. V, 168-169.

❖   ❖   ❖

As for the book of Genesis, the story of the creation found there is perhaps metaphorical; it ought therefore to be left to the theologians; and the creation ought not to be taken as divided into six days, but the division ought to be made only with regard to our manner of conceiving it, as St. Augustine did with his Thoughts on the Angels.

Burman. V, 169.

GEOMETRY

I hope to establish by demonstration which questions can be solved in such and such a way and not otherwise, with the result that nothing will be left to discover in geometry. The work, it is true, is infinite, and cannot be accomplished by one person alone. What an unbelievably ambitious project!

To Beeckman, Mar. 26, 1619. X, 157.

❖   ❖   ❖

I conceived the object of geometry as continuous body, or a space which was indefinitely extended in length, breadth, and height or depth, divisible into various parts, which could have various shapes and sizes, and be moved or transposed in all ways.

Discourse, IV. VI, 36.

❖   ❖   ❖

I know very well that the number of those who can understand my geometry will be very small.

Letter to Plempius, Oct. 3, 1637. I, 411.

GLANDS

It is with good reason that the *conarium* [pineal gland] is similar to a gland, because the principal role of all the glands is to receive the most subtle parts of the blood which are given off by the blood vessels around them, and the role of the *conarium* is to receive the animal spirits in the same way.

Letter to Mersenne, Dec. 24, 1640(?). III, 264.

GOD

When Genesis says that God separated light from darkness, it means that he separated the good angels from the evil ones. One cannot actually separate a privation from a positive quality, and it is for this reason that the text cannot be taken literally. God is pure intelligence.

Cogitationes Privatae. X, 218.

◇　◇　◇

If God is not conceived by the imagination, either one conceives nothing when one speaks of God (which would mark a shocking blindness), or one conceives him in some other manner.

Letter to Mersenne, July, 1641. III, 393.

◇　◇　◇

Although I do not doubt that everyone has the idea of God in him, at least implicitly, i.e., that he has in him the disposition to conceive the idea of God explicitly, I am not astonished nevertheless to see men who do not feel that they have this idea in them, or rather who do not perceive it and still will not perceive it, after having read my *Meditations,* if you wish, a thousand times.

Letter to "Hyperaspistas," Aug., 1641. III, 430-431.

◇　◇　◇

The idea by which I conceive a God who is sovereign, eternal, infinite, immutable, all-knowing, all-powerful, and universal Creator of all things which are not himself; this idea, I say, certainly has within it more objective reality than those by which finite substances are represented to me.

Meditations, III. IX, 32.

By the name "God" I understand a substance which is infinite, eternal, immutable, free, all-knowing, all-powerful, and by which I myself, and all other things which exist (if it is true that there are any other things which exist) have been created and produced.

Meditations, III. IX, 35-36.

❖   ❖   ❖

The unity, the simplicity, or the inseparability of all the things which are in God, is one of the principal perfections which I conceive to be in him.

Meditations, III. IX, 40.

❖   ❖   ❖

The existence of God is much more evident than that of any sensible thing.

Replies, I. IX, 85.

❖   ❖   ❖

Although God has always existed, nevertheless, because he himself actually conserves himself, it seems quite proper to call him the cause of himself.

Replies, I. IX, 87.

❖   ❖   ❖

The substance which we understand to be supremely perfect, and in which we conceive nothing which comprises any fault or limitation upon perfection, is called *God*.

Replies, II. IX, 125.

❖   ❖   ❖

The most perfect thing that we can conceive: this is what all men call *God*.

Letter to Clerselier. IX, 209.

❖   ❖   ❖

When one considers attentively the immensity of God, one sees that it is manifestly impossible that there is anything which does not depend upon him, not only of all that subsists, but also that there is neither order, nor law, nor measure of goodness and truth which does not depend upon him.

Replies, VI. IX, 235.

God can do all that we can comprehend clearly; and if there are other things which God is said not to be able to do, it is because they imply a contradiction in their ideas, i.e., they are not intelligible.

Letter to Regius, June, 1642. III, 567.

◈   ◈   ◈

Reflecting upon the idea that we have naturally [or innately] of him [God], we see that he is eternal, all-knowing, all-powerful, source of all goodness and truth, creator of all things, and finally that he has within him everything in which we can recognize some infinite perfection, or, better, that is not limited by any imperfection.

Principles, I, 22. IX2, 35.

◈   ◈   ◈

All the knowledge that we can have of God, without miracle, in this life, derives from reasoning and from the sequence of our words, which deduces it from the principles of the faith, which is obscure, or comes from natural ideas and notions which are in us, which, however clear they might be, are only clumsy and confused upon so high a subject.

Letter to Newcastle, Mar. or Apr., 1648. V, 136-137.

◈   ◈   ◈

Knowing by the idea of God that he is the most perfect being, to whom all the absolute perfections belong, I ought not to attribute to him anything that I have not recognized to be absolutely perfect; and everything that I can so imagine and conceive as an absolutely perfect perfection, simply from the fact that I can imagine it, belongs to the nature of God.

Burman. V, 158.

◈   ◈   ◈

One ought not to say of anything that it cannot be done by God; given that every species of truth and goodness depends upon his omnipotence, I would not even say that God could not make a mountain without a valley, or that one and two not make three.

Letter to Arnauld, July 29, 1648. V, 223-224.

75

I boldly assert that God can do everything tha⁺ I conceive
as possible, without having the temerity to say that he cannot
do what is inconsistent with my manner of conceiving.

Letter to More, Feb. 5, 1649. V, 272.

❖   ❖   ❖

See *being by itself.*

GOOD

If the understanding never represented anything to the will
as good, which was not good, then the will would never fail
to choose correctly.

Letter to Mersenne, May, 1637. I, 366.

❖   ❖   ❖

When the idea of the good is considered as a rule for our
actions, it is taken as all the perfection which there can be in
the thing which is called good, and it may be compared to a
straight line, which is unique among the infinity of curves, to
which evil may be compared. It is in this sense that the philosophers usually say that the good comes from the whole cause,
the evil from some defect. But when one considers the goods
and the evils which can be in the same thing, in order to
know what value to place upon it, as I did when I spoke of
the esteem which we ought to give to this life, one takes the
good to be everything from which he can have some benefit,
and one calls evil only that from which he can receive some
harm; for the other faults that might be there are not counted.

Letter to Elisabeth, Jan. 1646. IV, 354-355.

GRATITUDE

Gratitude is a species of love, excited in us by some action
of the person for whom we have it, and by which we believe
that he has done some good to us, or at least that he has had
the intention of doing so.

Passions, III, 193. XI, 473-474.

❖   ❖   ❖

See *favor.*

GRAVITY

See *fall; weight.*

GRAVITY, CENTER OF

The center of gravity is not fixed and immobile in each body, as the ancients supposed.

Treatise on Mechanics. I, 447.

❖   ❖   ❖

I could demonstrate that even the definition of the center of gravity, which was given by Archimedes, is false, and that there is no such center.

Letter to Mersenne, May 17, 1638. II, 142.

GROWTH

There are two sorts of growth. First, that of non-living beings, which do not partake of nourishment, in which growth takes place by means of the simple apposition of parts, without any change in those parts, and [second] that of living beings which partake of nourishment, in which growth always implies a certain change in the parts.

On Growth and Nutrition, Nov., 1637. XI, 596.

❖   ❖   ❖

See *fat.*

GUESSES

Everyone feels freer to guess at an obscure subject than one which is evident, and it is much easier to have some vague notion about any subject, no matter what, than to arrive at the real truth about a single question, however simple that may be.

Rules, II. X, 365.

H

HAPPINESS

Happiness depends only on things which are outside ourselves, from which it follows that those persons are esteemed happier than sages, to whom some good happens that they have not obtained for themselves, where blessedness consists, it seems to me, in a perfect contentment of mind and an internal satisfaction, which those who are most favored by fortune do not ordinarily have, and which the sages acquire without the help of fortune.

Letter to Elisabeth, Aug. 4, 1645. IV, 264.

◇　◇　◇

The greatest happiness of man depends upon the right use of reason, and as a result, the study by which he acquires it is the most useful occupation that he can have, as it is also doubtless the most agreeable and the sweetest.

Letter to Elisabeth, Aug. 4, 1645. IV, 267.

HARDNESS

Hardness, or resistance to division, depends upon the quantity [of material in a particle]; and, on the other hand, the extent of the surface area facilitates division.

Letter to Mersenne, Dec., 1640. III, 256.

◇　◇　◇

As for hardness, we know nothing more about it, by means of touch, than that the particles of hard bodies resist the motion of our hands when they come together; but if, every time that we moved our hands toward some part of the body, the bodies which were in that place moved back as quickly as our hands approached, it is certain that we would never sense hardness.

Principles, II, 4. IX2, 65.

HASTE

Actually, one often sees people who throw themselves into the examination of problems with so much haste, that they give their vagabond minds the job of finding a solution, before they have asked how a solution might be recognized, if they stumbled upon one by accident.

Rules, XIII. X, 434.

HATE

Seeing that love, however perverse it may be, always has the good as its object, it does not seem to me that it can much corrupt our morals, as can hate, which intends nothing but evil.

Letter to Chanut, Feb. 1, 1647. IV, 613-614.

❖   ❖   ❖

Hate is an emotion caused by the [animal] spirits, which incites the soul to want to be separated from objects which present themselves to it as harmful.

Passions, II, 79. XI, 387.

❖   ❖   ❖

In hate, the pulse is irregular and weaker, and often more rapid; one feels flashes of cold, intermixed with an indefinable biting and prickling heat in the chest; the stomach no longer does its work, and is inclined to vomit and reject the food that has been eaten, or at least to corrupt it and convert it into bad humors.

Passions, II, 98. XI, 402.

❖   ❖   ❖

Since hate and sadness ought to be rejected by the soul, even when they come from true knowledge, for an even greater reason they ought to be rejected when they come from some false opinion.

Passions, II, 142. XI, 434.

❖   ❖   ❖

See *love*.

HEALTH

The conservation of health has always been the principal goal of my studies.

Letter to Newcastle, Oct., 1645. IV, 329.

HEARING

The fourth [external sense] is hearing, which has as its object only various vibrations of the air; for there are nerves underneath the ears, attached to three small bones, which are attached to one another; the first is held against the small membrane which covers the concavity which is called the ear drum, in such a way that all the various vibrations which the air from outside communicates to that membrane are communicated to the soul by these nerves, and thus make it hear the various sounds.

Principles, IV, 194. IX2, 314.

HEART

The flesh of the heart contains in its pores one of the fires without light, about which I have spoken above, which makes it so hot and so ardent, that as soon as blood enters into one of the two chambers or concavities in it, the blood promptly swells, and dilates.

Treatise on Man. XI, 123.

❖ ❖ ❖

It is so important to know the true cause of the movement of the heart that without this knowledge it is impossible to know anything concerning the theory of medicine, because all the other functions of the animal depend upon it.

Description of Human Body, II. XI, 245.

❖ ❖ ❖

The heart is the source of the passions, since it prepares the blood and the [animal] spirits which produce them.

Passions, II, 114. XI, 413.

HEAT

As for heat, the sensation that we have of it, I think, can be taken as a species of pain, when it is violent, and sometimes as a species of pleasurable sensation, when it is moderate.

The World, II. XI, 9-10.

❖ ❖ ❖

As for heat, I do not believe it to be the same thing as light, nor the rarefaction of air; but I conceive it as a wholly different thing, which can often proceed from light, and from which rarefaction can proceed.

Letter to Mersenne, June or July, 1635. I, 323-324.

❖ ❖ ❖

I suppose here that, as for cold and heat, there is no need to conceive anything other than that the tiny particles of bodies which touch us are agitated more or less strongly than usual.

Meteorology, I. VI, 235-236.

❖ ❖ ❖

You can know by experience that heat consists of the agitation of the tiny particles of earthly bodies.

Meteorology, II. VI, 245.

❖ ❖ ❖

As for heat, even though it can be caused by the agitation of the particles of subtle matter, generally it consists properly only in the agitation of the earth particles, because these have more force for moving the particles of other bodies and thus to burn them.

Letter to Mersenne, Jan. 9, 1639. II, 485.

❖ ❖ ❖

An agitation of the tiny particles of terrestrial bodies is called heat in them (whether it has been excited by the light of the sun, or by some other cause), principally when it is greater than is customary, and when it can fairly strongly move the nerves of our hands, so that it can be sensed; because the name heat is used in connection with the sense of touch.

Principles, IV, 29. IX2, 215.

❖ ❖ ❖

Heat is the most powerful agent that we know in nature.

Description of Human Body, II. XI, 244.

HISTORY

By [mathematical] history I understand all that has been discovered and which is found in books.

Letter to Hogelande, Feb. 8, 1640.

❖ ❖ ❖

See *Learning.*

HOPE

It is enough to think that acquisition of a good or flight from an evil is possible, to be incited to desire it. But when one considers, in addition, that it seems more or less likely that one may obtain what one desires, that which represents to us that it is likely, excites hope in us, and that which represents that it is unlikely, excites fear, of which jealousy is a species. When the hope is extreme, its nature changes, and is called security or assurance. As, on the contrary, extreme fear becomes despair.

Passions, II, 58. XI, 375.

❖ ❖ ❖

Hope is a disposition of the soul to persuade itself that what it desires will happen, which is caused by a particular movement of the [animal] spirits, namely by that of joy and desire mixed together.

Passions, III, 165. XI, 456.

HORROR

Horror is instituted by nature to represent to the soul a sudden and unforeseen death: in such a way that, even though it is sometimes only the touch of a worm or the noise of a trembling leaf, or its shadow, which causes horror, as much emotion is sensed at first as if a very evident threat of death was offered to the senses. This suddenly gives birth to an agitation which leads the soul to employ all its forces to avoid so imminent an evil.

Passions, II, 89. XI, 394-395.

HUMILITY

Virtuous humility consists only in the fact that the reflection which we make upon the infirmity of our nature, and upon the mistakes that we might once have committed, or are capable of committing, which are no fewer than those which others might commit, leads us to think of ourselves as no better than another, and makes us think that, since others have their free will as well as we do, that they can use it equally well.

Passions, III, 155. XI, 447.

83

HUMOR

See *joyous humor, sad humor, choleric humor.*

HUNGER

When the liquids, which, as I said above, serve as *aqua fortis* in the stomach, and enter there without stopping, from all the blood from the ends of the arteries, find that there is not enough food to dissolve to keep them occupied, they turn against the stomach itself, and irritating the tiny threads of its nerves more strongly than usual, cause movements in the particles of the brain from which the nerves come. This will be the cause, when the soul is united to the body, for it to conceive the general idea of *hunger.*

Treatise on Man. XI, 163.

❖ ❖ ❖

I am persuaded that hunger and thirst are sensed in the same way as colors, sounds, odors, and generally all the objects of the external senses, that is by means of nerves, which are extended like tiny threads from the brain to all the other parts of the body.

Letter to Newcastle, Oct., 1645. IV, 326.

HYPOTHESIS

I desire that what I write [here] be taken solely as a hypothesis, which can be quite distant from the truth; but even if it is, I will believe that I have done a great deal, if everything that is deduced from it conforms entirely with experience: for if that is the case, it will not be less useful for living than if it were true, because it could be used in the same way to arrange natural causes to produce the desired effects.

Principles, II, 44. IX2, 123.

I

IDEAS

The common sense functions like a seal, which imprints the figures or ideas, which come to it in a pure and incorporeal form from the external senses, in the phantasy or imagination, which is like wax.

Rules, XII. X, 414.

❖ ❖ ❖

Although everyone commonly believes that the ideas which we have in our thought are entirely similar to the objects from which they proceed, I do not see any reason to believe this; but I notice, on the contrary, many experiments which ought to make us doubt it.

The World, I. XI, 3-4.

❖ ❖ ❖

Those [figures] which are traced by the [animal] spirits upon the surface of the [pineal] gland, *which is the seat of the imagination, and of the common sense,* ought to be taken to be the *ideas,* that is for the forms or images which the rational soul considers immediately, when, after it has been united to this machine [the body], it imagines or senses some object.

Treatise on Man. XI, 176-177.

❖ ❖ ❖

Note that I say: imagine or sense; since I want to understand generally, under the name *Idea* all the impressions that the [animal] spirits can receive when they emerge from the [pineal] gland, all of which are attributed to the common sense, when they depend upon the presence of their objects; but they can also proceed from many other causes, as I will explain to you later, and then they are to be attributed to the imagination.

Treatise on Man. XI, 177.

◈　◈　◈

There need not be, in all this, any resemblance between the ideas that it [the soul] conceives and the movements [of the nerves] which cause these ideas.

Dioptrics, VI. VI, 131.

◈　◈　◈

Since our ideas can receive their forms and their existence only from certain external objects or from ourselves, they can represent only the reality or perfection which is in these objects or in ourselves.

Letter to Vatier, Feb. 22, 1638. I, 560-561.

◈　◈　◈

Among the ideas, some seem to me to be born with me [innate], others to be foreign and to come from outside me [adventitious], and others to be made and invented by me [factitious or fictitious].

Meditations, III. IX, 29.

◈　◈　◈

I find in my mind two completely different ideas of the sun: one takes its origin in the senses, and ought to be placed in the category of those which I said come from outside myself, according to which the sun appears to me to be extremely small; the other idea is derived from the reasons of astronomy, i.e., from certain innate notions, or perhaps is formed by myself in some way or another, according to which it appears to me to be several times larger than all the earth.

Meditations, III. IX, 31.

◈　◈　◈

Every idea being a work of the mind, its nature is such that it requires no other formal reality than that which it receives and borrows from the thought or the mind, of which it is only a mode, i.e., a manner or fashion of thinking.

Meditations, III. IX, 32.

◈　◈　◈

The natural light makes me know with certainty that ideas are within me like pictures or images which can, truly, easily fall short of the perfection of the things from which they have been derived but which can never contain anything greater or more perfect.

Meditations, III. IX, 33.

By the word *idea,* I understand everything that can be in our thought, and I have distinguished three sorts of them: namely, some are *adventitious,* like the ordinary idea of the sun; some are constructed [*factae*] or *factitious,* to which rank one can assign those that the astronomers have of the sun, through their reasoning; and others are *innate,* like the idea of God, of the soul, of body, of the triangle, and in general all those which represent true, immutable and eternal essences.

Letter to Mersenne, June 16, 1641. III, 383.

❖   ❖   ❖

I do not call only the images which are painted in the imagination by the name "idea"; on the contrary, I do not call them by that name at all, so long as they are in the corporeal imagination; but I generally call everything that is in our mind by the name "idea," whenever we conceive a thing, in whatever manner we conceive it.

Letter to Mersenne, July, 1641. III, 392-393.

❖   ❖   ❖

If he [an uknown author] wishes to take the word *idea* in the way that I have said quite expressly that I take it, without stopping at the equivocation of those who restrict the word to the images of material things which are formed in the imagination, it will be easy for him to recognize that, by the idea of God, I understand nothing other than what every man usually means when he speaks of God.

Letter to Mersenne, July, 1641. III, 393.

❖   ❖   ❖

Everything that we conceive without an image is a purely mental idea, and everything that we conceive with an image is an idea of the imagination.

Letter to Mersenne, July, 1641. III, 395.

In the word *idea* there is an equivocation: either it can be taken materially as an operation of my understanding, and in this sense one cannot say that it is more perfect than I am; or it can be taken objectively [i.e., in terms of its object] for the thing which is represented by that operation, which, even though it is not supposed to exist outside of my understanding, can nevertheless be more perfect than I am, by reason of its essence.

Meditations, Preface. VII, 8.

❖   ❖   ❖

The idea is the thing itself, as it is conceived or thought, insofar as it is objectively in the understanding.

Replies, I. IX, 81.

❖   ❖   ❖

By the word *idea* I understand that form of each of our thoughts, by the immediate perception of which we have knowledge of these thoughts. In such a way that I cannot express anything by words when I understand what I am saying except from the fact that there is in me the idea of the thing which is signified by my words. And thus I do not only give the name idea to the images which are depicted in my imagination; on the contrary, I do not call them by that name at all, insofar as they are in the corporeal imagination, i.e., insofar as they are depicted in some parts of the brain, but solely insofar as they inform the mind itself, when it applies itself to that part of the brain.

Replies, II. IX, 124.

❖   ❖   ❖

I take the name idea to mean all that is immediately conceived by the mind. So that, when I will and when I fear, because I simultaneously conceive that I will and that I fear, this act of will and this fear are included by me among the ideas; and I make use of this word, because it was commonly taken by philosophers to signify the forms of the conceptions of the divine understanding, even though we do not recognize in God any *phantasia* or corporeal imagination; and I did not know any word that would be more proper.

Replies, III. IX, 141.

❖   ❖   ❖

If one has no idea [of God], that is, no perception which corresponds to the signification of the word *God,* then one says in vain that he believes that *God* exists.

Letter to Clerselier. IX, 210.

❖   ❖   ❖

[Concerning] the idea of God, it should be noted that it is not a case of the essence of the idea according to which it is only a mode existing in the soul (this mode being no more perfect than the man), but it is a case of objective perfection, which the principles of metaphysics teach as being contained formally or eminently in its cause.

Letter to Regius, June, 1642. III, 566.

❖   ❖   ❖

I do not introduce any difference between the soul and its ideas, other than as between a piece of wax and the various shapes which it can receive.

Letter to Mesland, May 2, 1644(?). IV, 113.

❖   ❖   ❖

As it is not properly an action, but a passion of the wax, to receive various shapes, it seems to me that it is also a passion in the soul to receive such or such an idea, and that there are only its volitions which are actions; and its ideas are placed in it, partly by the objects which touch the senses, partly by the impressions which are in the brain, and partly also by the dispositions which have preceded these in the soul itself, and by the movements of its will; as the wax receives its shapes, partly from other bodies which press into it, partly from the shapes or other qualities which are already in it, as from the fact that it is more or less heavy or soft, etc., and partly also from its motion, when it has been moved and has in itself the force to continue to move itself.

Letter to Mesland, May 2, 1644(?). IV, 113-114.

In addition [to ideas which represent things] there are the ideas of common notions, which are not ideas of things properly speaking; but then *idea* is taken in a larger sense.

Burman. V, 153.

❖   ❖   ❖

See *impressions; materially; formally; will.*

IDEAS, ADVENTITIOUS

[I do not] say that all ideas are innate, but that there are also adventitious ideas, as for example the ideas of the city of Leiden, the city of Alkmaar, etc.

Burman. V, 165.

IDEAS, INNATE

I hold that all those [ideas] which include neither affirmation nor negation are *innate* for us; for the sense organs bring nothing to us which is like the idea which is aroused in us at their occasion, and thus this idea must have been in us previously.

Letter to Mersenne, July 23, 1641. III, 418.

❖   ❖   ❖

When I consider which figures can be inscribed in a circle, it is not at all necessary that I think that every figure which has four sides is among them; on the contrary, I cannot even pretend that this is so, as long as I refuse to consider any thoughts which I cannot conceive clearly and distinctly. And as a consequence there is a great difference between false suppositions, like this one, and the truly innate ideas, of which the first and principal idea is that of God.

Meditations, V. IX, 54.

❖   ❖   ❖

When I say that some idea is innate, or that it is naturally imprinted in our souls, I do not understand that it is always present to our thought, because then there would be no innate ideas; but simply that we have in us the faculty of producing it.

Replies, III. IX, 147.

90

◈   ◈   ◈

I never wrote or concluded that the mind required innate ideas which were in some way different from its faculty of thinking; but when I observed the existence in me of certain thoughts which proceeded, not from extraneous objects nor from the determination of my will, but solely from the faculty of thinking which is within me, then, that I might distinguish the ideas or notions (which are the forms of these thoughts) from other thoughts *adventitious* or *factitious*, I termed the former *innate*. In the same sense we say that in some families generosity is innate, in others certain diseases like gout or gravel, not that on this account the babes of these families suffer from these diseases in their mother's womb, but because they are born with a certain disposition or propensity for contracting them.

Notes against a Program, XII.

◈   ◈   ◈

See *seeds of truth, seeds of thought; perfection.*

IDENTITY

The surface [of the Host at the Sacrament] remains numerically the same as that which existed previously between the air and the bread, because it does not take its numerical identity from the identity of bodies in which it exists, but solely from the identity or resemblance of the dimensions: as we can say that the Loire is the same river which existed ten years ago, even though it is not the same water and though perhaps also there is no particle of the same earth which surrounded that water.

Letter to Mesland, Feb. 9, 1644. IV, 164-165.

IMAGES

One must not suppose that, in order to sense, the soul must contemplate some images which are sent by the objects to the brain, as our philosophers commonly say; or, at least, one must conceive the nature of these images quite differently from them.

Dioptrics, IV. VI, 112.

There are no images which completely resemble the objects which they represent: for otherwise there would be no distinction between the object and its image: but it suffices for them to resemble their object in a few things.

Dioptrics, IV. VI, 113.

❖ ❖ ❖

The images of objects are not formed only at the back of the eye, but they also pass from there to the brain.

Dioptrics, V. VI, 128.

IMAGINATION

In order to make use of the assistance of the imagination, we must note that every time that one deduces something which is unknown from some other thing which is already known, one never discovers a new type of being; the process of knowledge only permits us to see that the thing for which we are searching participates, in some way or another, in the nature of those things which are given in the problem.

Rules, XIV. X, 438.

❖ ❖ ❖

The imagination itself, with the ideas which exist in it, is nothing other than a real, veritable body, with extension and figure.

Rules, XIV. X, 441.

❖ ❖ ❖

I am currently dissecting the heads of various animals, in order to explain what imagination, memory, etc., consist of.

Letter to Mersenne, Nov.-Dec., 1632. I, 263.

❖ ❖ ❖

It seems to me that those who want to use their imagination in order to comprehend [the ideas of God and the soul] do the same as those who want to use their eyes in order to hear sounds or smell odors.

Discourse, IV. VI, 37.

❖ ❖ ❖

The imagination [is] that which can variously change the

ideas and compose new ideas out of them, and, by the same means, distribute the animal spirits in the muscles so as to make the limbs and the body move in so many various ways.

Discourse, V. VI, 55.

❖ ❖ ❖

The part of the mind which helps most in mathematics, namely the imagination, hinders more than it helps in metaphysical speculations.

Letter to Mersenne, Nov. 13, 1639. II, 622.

❖ ❖ ❖

When I consider attentively what the imagination is, I find that it is nothing other than a certain application of the faculty of knowing, to the body which is intimately present to it, and which therefore exists.

Meditations, VI. IX, 57.

❖ ❖ ❖

I have need of a particular intense application of mind, in order to imagine, which I do not use in order to conceive; and that particular application of the mind shows clearly the difference there is between imagination, and intellection or pure conception.

Meditations, VI. IX, 58.

❖ ❖ ❖

In order to imagine, for example, a pentagon, there is need of a particular contention of the mind which gives us that figure (that is, its five sides and the space that they enclose) as present, which we do not use for conceiving.

Replies, III. IX, 139.

❖ ❖ ❖

See *intellection; tablet, blank.*

IMAGINE

To imagine is nothing other than to contemplate the shape or the image of a corporeal thing.

Meditations, II. IX, 22.

❖ ❖ ❖

See *consider.*

93

IMAGINING

Imagining is a way of thinking which is appropriate for material things.

Discourse, IV. VI, 37.

◈　◈　◈

The faculties of imagining and of sensing belong to the soul, because they are species of thoughts; and nevertheless they only belong to the soul insofar as it is joined to the body, because they are the sort of thoughts without which one can conceive the soul completely pure.

Letter to Gibieuf, Jan. 19, 1642. III, 479.

IMMORTALITY

I have not written a word [in the *Meditations*] about the immortality of the soul, but you should not be astonished about that; for I would not know how to demonstrate that God could not annihilate it, but only to show that it is of a nature entirely distinct from that of the body, and as a consequence that it is not naturally subject to death with the body, which is all that is required to establish religion; and it is also all that I proposed to prove.

Letter to Mersenne, Dec. 24, 1640(?). III, 265-266.

◈　◈　◈

The human body can easily perish, but the mind or the soul of man (which I do not distinguish) is immortal by its very nature.

Meditations, Summary. IX, 10.

◈　◈　◈

I confess that I have nothing to say in reply [to the objection that immortality is not proved in the *Meditations*]; for I do not have so much presumption as to attempt to determine, by the force of human reasoning, a thing which depends only on the pure will of God.

Replies, II. IX, 120.

IMMUTABILITY

What foundation could one find which is more firm and solid, upon which to establish a truth, what could one wish

94

for, than to take the firmness and the immutability which is in God?

The World, VII. XI, 43.

IMPENETRABILITY

Impenetrability belongs to the essence of the extended, and not to the essence of anything else.

Letter to More, Apr. 15, 1649. V, 342.

IMPOSSIBILITY

All impossibility, or, if I may make use here of the word of the School, all *implicantia,* consists solely in our concept or thought, which cannot conjoin ideas which are contrary to one another; and impossibility cannot consist in anything which is beyond the understanding, because, simply from the fact that it is beyond the understanding, it is manifest that it does not imply anything, but that it is possible.

Replies, II. IX, 119.

IMPRESSIONS

I conceive that various impressions are formed in the brain [of animals], some by external objects which move the senses, others by the internal dispositions of the body, or by the vestiges of preceding impressions which have remained in the memory, or by the agitation of spirits which come from the heart, or also in man by the action of the soul, which has some power to change the impressions which are in the brain, as, reciprocally, these impressions have the power to excite thoughts in the soul which do not depend upon the will.

Letter to Elisabeth, Oct. 6, 1645. IV, 310.

IMPUDENCE

Impudence or effrontery, which is a scorn of shame, and often also of pride, is not a passion, because there is in us no particular movement of the [animal] spirits which excites it; but it is a vice opposed to shame, and also to pride, insofar as one or the other of these is good, just as ingratitude is opposed to gratitude, and cruelty to pity.

Passions, III, 207. XI, 483.

IMPULSE

A person may be said to believe on impulse if he judges things by some spontaneous belief, without having been convinced by any reasoning.

Rules, XII. X, 424.

INCLINATIONS

I cannot conceive of natural inclinations except in something which has understanding, and I do not even attribute it to animals which do not have reason; but I explain everything that we call natural appetites or inclinations in them solely by the rules of mechanics.

Letter to Mersenne, Oct. 28, 1640. III, 213.

❖   ❖   ❖

When I say that these little balls [i.e., the particles of light] make some effort, or rather that they have the inclination, to move away from the centers about which they revolve, I do not understand that one attributes to them any thought from which that inclination proceeds, but only that they are so situated and disposed to move that they would actually move away, if they were not held back by any other cause.

Principles, III, 56. IX2, 131.

INDECISION

Indecision is another species of fear, which keeps the soul as though it were in balance, among many actions that it could perform, and thus keeps it from doing any of them, giving it time to choose before it decides.

Passions, III, 170. XI, 459.

INDEFINITE

I here make a distinction between *indefinite* and *infinite*. And there is nothing which I call properly infinite, except that in which I do not find limits in any parts, in which sense God alone is infinite. But the things which I simply see no end to, under some consideration, like the extension of imaginary spaces, the multitude of numbers, the divisibility of the part of a quantity, and other similar things, I call simply *indefinite*, and not *infinite*, because they are not without end or limits in every part.

Replies, I. IX, 89-90

When we see things in which, in a certain sense, we do not notice any limits, we will not be certain for that reason that they are infinite, but we will simply say that they are indefinite.

Principles, I, 26. IX2, 36.

◇　◇　◇

I do not say that the world is *infinite,* but *indefinite* only. In which there is a quite notable difference: for, to say that a thing is infinite, one ought to have some reason which makes it known as such, of a sort that one can have of God alone; but to say that a thing is indefinite, it suffices to have no reason by which one can prove that it has limits.

Letter to Chanut, June 6, 1647. V, 51.

INDIFFERENCE

Although I have written that indifference is rather a fault than a perfection in our own freedom, it does not follow from that that it is the same in God.

Letter to Mersenne, Apr. 21, 1641. III, 360.

◇　◇　◇

A total indifference in God is a very great proof of his omnipotence.

Replies, VI. IX, 233.

◇　◇　◇

Indifference seems to me properly to signify the state of the will when it is not impelled in one direction rather than in another by the perception of the true or the good; and it is in this sense that I took it when I wrote that the lowest degree of freedom is that in which we determine ourselves to things about which we are indifferent.

Letter to Mesland, Feb. 9, 1645. IV, 173.

INDIFFERENT

I have not said that man was indifferent only where he lacks knowledge; but rather that he is all the more indifferent as he knows fewer reasons which impel him to choose one side rather than the other.

Letter to Mesland, May 2, 1644(?). IV, 115.

See *free.*

INDIGNATION

The evil done by others, when it is not related to us, only makes us indignant toward them; and when it is related to us, it also excites anger.

Passions, II, 65. XI, 378.

◈   ◈   ◈

Indignation is a species of hate or aversion, which one has naturally against those who do some evil, of whatever nature it might be.

Passions, III, 195. XI, 475.

INDUCTION

See *enumeration.*

INDUCTION, MATHEMATICAL

When a deduction is complex and involved, we give it the name of enumeration or [mathematical] induction, because the understanding cannot then include it all in the same instant, but its certainty depends in some way upon memory, which must retain the judgments concerning each of the parts of the enumeration, so that a single conclusion can be derived from all of them together.

Rules, XI. X, 408.

INERTIA

I do not recognize any inertia or natural resistance to motion in bodies, any more than does M. Mydorge, and believe that, when only one man walks, he makes the whole mass of the earth move ever so little, because he weighs it down, now in one place, and afterward in another.

Letter to Huygens, Dec. 1638. II, 466-467.

INERTIA, NATURAL

The more matter a body contains, the more *natural inertia* it has.

Letter to Debeaune, Apr. 30, 1639. II, 543.

INFANCY

The mind in infancy is so caught up in the body that it has no thoughts other than those which derive from its attachment to the body.

Burman. V, 150.

INFINITE

I have never discussed the infinite except to submit myself to it, and not to determine what it is or is not.

Letter to Mersenne, Jan. 28, 1641. III, 293.

❖　❖　❖

That by which the infinite differs from the finite is real and positive, and the limitation by which the finite differs from the infinite is a nonentity or a negation of being.

Letter to "Hyperaspistas," Aug., 1641. III, 427.

❖　❖　❖

The infinite, insofar as it is infinite, is not actually comprehended, but nevertheless it is understood.

Replies, I. IX, 89.

❖　❖　❖

To understand clearly and distinctly that a thing is such that one cannot find limits to it, is clearly to understand that it is infinite.

Replies, I. IX, 89.

❖　❖　❖

We will call these [material] things indefinite rather than infinite, in order to reserve to God alone the word infinite; because we do not notice any limits upon his perfections, and also because we are completely sure that there cannot be any limits.

Principles, I, 27. IX2, 37.

❖　❖　❖

As for ourselves, we can never find any limit whatever in these things [number, quantity, etc.], and thus, from our point of view, they are indefinite, or better, infinite without doubt, for the indefinite, repeatedly multiplied, as is here the case, is

99

the infinite itself. And thus, perhaps we can say that the world is infinite; the same for number, etc. But, from the point of view of God, perhaps he conceives and comprehends determinate limits to the world, to number, to quantity, and perhaps he comprehends something greater than the world, than number, etc., which will thus be finite for him.

Burmàn. V, 167.

❖   ❖   ❖

I would not dare to say that [the world] is infinite, because I conceive that God is greater than the world, not because of his extent, which I do not conceive in God, as I have said many times, but because of his perfection.

Letter to More, Apr. 15, 1649. V, 344.

❖   ❖   ❖

See *indefinite*.

INGRATITUDE

As for ingratitude, it is not a passion: for nature has not placed in us any motion of the [animal] spirits which excites it; but it is solely a vice directly opposed to gratitude, insofar as the latter is always virtuous and one of the principal links of human society.

Passions, III, 194. XI, 474.

INSTANT

The word instant excludes only temporal priority.

Letter to Mersenne, May 17, 1638. II, 143.

INSTINCTS

I distinguish two sorts of instincts: one is in us insofar as we are men and is purely intellectual; this is the natural light or *intuitus mentis* [mental intuition], in which alone I hold that men should trust; the other is in us insofar as we are animals, and is a certain natural impulsion for the conservation of our body, for the enjoyment of corporeal pleasures, etc., which ought not always to be followed.

Letter to Mersenne, Oct. 16, 1639. II, 599.

INTELLECT

See *understanding*.

INTELLECTION

[Imagination] differs from pure intellection solely in that the mind, when conceiving [i.e., using pure intellection] turns in some way toward itself, and considers one of the ideas that it has; but in imagining, it turns toward the body, and considers something there which conforms to the idea that it has formed by itself or which it has received through the senses.

Meditations, VI. IX, 58.

INTELLECTUAL NATURE

The idea of intellectual nature in general, when considered as without limitation, is that which represents God to us, and when considered as limited, is that of an Angel or a human soul.

Letter to °°°, May, 1637. I, 353.

INTENTIONAL SPECIES

When I see a stick, it is not necessary to imagine that little images come from it, flying through the air, commonly called intentional species, which pass to my eye, but only that the rays of light reflected from the stick excite some movements in the optic nerve, and, by means of them, in the brain itself.

Replies, VI. IX, 236-237.

INTUITION

Concerning the objects which are proposed for our study, it is necessary to seek out, not what others have thought, or what we ourselves conjecture, but that of which we can have a clear and evident intuition, or what we can deduce with certainty.

Rules, III. X, 366.

◈   ◈   ◈

By *intuition* I understand, not the fluctuating testimony of the senses, nor the misleading judgment that proceeds from the blundering constructions of imagination, but the conception which an unclouded and attentive mind gives us so readily and distinctly that we are wholly freed from doubt about what we

101

understand. Or, what comes to the same thing, *intuition* is the undoubting conception of an unclouded and attentive mind, and springs from the light of reason alone; it is more certain than deduction itself, in that it is simpler, though deduction, as we have noted above, cannot be erroneously conducted by us.

Rules, III. X, 368.

❖   ❖   ❖

We distinguish *intuition* of the mind from certain *deduction,* in that in the latter we may conceive a sort of movement or succession, but not in the former; and because, in addition, for deduction, unlike intuition, there is no need of actual, present experience, since deductions borrow their certitude, in some fashion, from memory.

Rules, III. X, 370.

❖   ❖   ❖

The manner in which we must use intellectual intuition becomes apparent to us when we compare it with the vision of the eyes.

Rules, IX. X, 401.

❖   ❖   ❖

In order to speak of intellectual intuition, we require two elements: first, that the proposition be comprehended clearly and distinctly; and second, that it be comprehended completely in a single moment, and not in several successive moments.

Rules, XI. X, 407.

❖   ❖   ❖

There can be no error in intuition alone, whether the things which are intuited are simple or composite.

Rules, XIII. X, 432.

❖   ❖   ❖

Intuitive knowledge is an elucidation of the mind, by which it sees those things in the light of God, which it pleases him to show it, by a direct impression of the divine light upon our understanding, which in this case is not considered as an agent, but solely as receiving the rays of divinity.

Letter to Newcastle, Mar. or Apr., 1648. V, 136.

See *instinct*.

INVENTION

When I was a youth, with a view to ingenious discoveries, I asked myself if I would not be able to invent for myself, without depending upon reading from any author. From that time on, little by little, I perceived that I proceeded according to determinate rules.

Cogitationes Privatae. X, 214.

❖　❖　❖

One cannot conceive a thing so well, and make it his own, when he learns it from someone else, as when he invents it himself.

Discourse, VI. VI, 69.

IRON

We do not have any [metal other than iron or steel] which bows less easily to the hammer, without the aid of the fire, which is made to melt with so much trouble, or which can be made so hard, without the mixture of any other body.

Principles, IV, 136. IX2, 273.

J

JEALOUSY

Jealousy is a species of fear, which is connected with the desire to keep possession of some good; and it does not come so much from the force of reasons, which make one judge that it can be lost, as from the great esteem that he has for it, which leads him to examine even the smallest subjects of suspicion, which are taken to be quite considerable reasons.

Passions, III, 167. XI, 457.

❖ ❖ ❖

People despise a man who is jealous of his wife, because it is evidence that he does not love her rightly, and that he has a bad opinion of himself or of her. I say that he does not love her rightly; for, if he had a true love for her, he would have no inclination not to have faith in her. But it is not properly she that he loves, it is only the good that he imagines consists in having sole possession of her; and he would not be afraid of losing this good, if he did not judge that he was not worthy of it, or that his wife was unfaithful.

Passions, III, 169. XI, 458-459.

JOY

When the blood which goes into the heart is purer and thinner, and burns there more readily than usual, it moves the tiny nerve there in the way that is required to cause the sensation of *joy*.

Treatise on Man. XI, 164-165.

❖ ❖ ❖

When it happens that our blood is quite pure and well tempered, in such a way that it dilates in the heart more easily and to a greater extent than usual, this stretches the little nerves which are at the entrances to its chambers, and moves them in a certain way, which reaches up to the brain, and there excites our soul naturally to sense joy.

Principles, IV, 190. IX2, 311.

❖   ❖   ❖

If I thought that the sovereign good were joy, I would not doubt that one ought to try to make himself joyous, at whatever price that might be, and I would approve the brute-like way in which some people drown their sorrows in wine, or benumb them with tobacco.

Letter to Elisabeth, Oct. 6, 1645. IV, 305.

❖   ❖   ❖

Internal joy has some secret power to render fortune more favorable.

Letter to Elisabeth, Nov., 1646. IV, 529.

❖   ❖   ❖

The consideration of a present good excites joy in us, and that of evil, sadness, when it is a good or an evil which is represented to us as pertaining to us.

Passions, II, 61. XI, 376.

❖   ❖   ❖

Joy is an agreeable emotion of the soul, which consists of the enjoyment that the soul has in the good, which the impressions in the brain represent to it as its own.

Passions, II, 91. XI, 396.

❖   ❖   ❖

Purely intellectual joy comes in the soul by the action only of the soul, and can be said to be a delightful emotion excited in it by itself, consisting in the enjoyment that it has of the good which its understanding represents to it as its own.

Passions, II, 91. XI, 397.

❖   ❖   ❖

In joy, the pulse is regular and faster than ordinary, but it is not so strong or so great as in love; and an agreeable warmth is felt; not only is it in the chest, but it also expands into all the external parts of the body, with the blood seen to flow in abundance; and nevertheless one loses his appetite, because the digestion is poorer than usual.

Passions, II, 99. XI, 402-403.

❖   ❖   ❖

Even a false joy is worth more than a sadness whose cause is true.

Passions, II, 142. XI, 435.

JOYOUS HUMOR

The *joyous humor* is composed of promptness and tranquility of mind; and goodness and confidence serve to render it more perfect.

Treatise on Man. XI, 167.

JOYS

The great joys are ordinarily sober and serious, and it is only the mediocre and passing joys which are accompanied by laughter.

Letter to Elisabeth, Oct. 6, 1645. IV, 305.

JUDGE

It seems to me that there can be only two things required for being always inclined to judge well: one is the knowledge of the truth, and the other, the habit of remembering and acquiescing in that knowledge, every time that the occasion requires it.

Letter to Elisabeth, Sept. 15, 1645. IV, 291.

JUDGMENTS

When men judge that space, which they call void, is nothing, they conceive it nevertheless as a positive thing; and when they think that accidental properties of things are real, they represent them to themselves as substances, even though they do not judge that they are substances, and thus, often, in many things the judgments of men differ from their perceptions.

Letter to "Hyperaspistas," Aug., 1641. III, 431.

❖   ❖   ❖

If often happens that the judgments of men are quite different from their perception or apprehension.

Letter to "Hyperaspistas," Aug., 1641. III, 432.

When I saw that, over and above perception, which is required as a basis for judgment, there must needs be affirmation,
or negation, to constitute the form of the judgment, and that it
is frequently open to us to withhold our assent, even if we
perceive a thing, I referred the act of judging, which consists
in nothing but *assent,* i.e. affirmation or negation, not to the
perception of the understanding, but to the determination of
the will.

Notes against a Program, XVI. VIII 2, 363.

❖   ❖   ❖

Judgment is assuredly the work of the will, and, insofar as
it is such, it is perfect; all imperfection from which it suffers
has its origin in the ignorance of the understanding; if that
ignorance can be made to disappear, hesitation would be made
to disappear also, and judgment would be constant and perfect.

Burman. V, 159.

K

KNOWING, POWER OF

The power by which we may, properly speaking, be said to know things, is a purely spiritual power, and is not less distinct from the body, taken altogether, than blood is from bone, or hand from eye.

Rules, XII. X, 415.

KNOWLEDGE

There is nothing more useful than to seek out the nature and limits of human knowledge.

Rules, VIII. X, 397.

❖ ❖ ❖

Concerning the knowledge of things only two points are to be considered: we who know, and the things themselves which are to be known.

Rules, XII. X, 411.

❖ ❖ ❖

Knowledge of the truth is like health of the soul: when you have it, you think no more about it.

Letter to Chanut, Mar. 31, 1649. V, 327.

❖ ❖ ❖

See *science*.

KNOWLEDGE, ADEQUATE

The author himself does not claim that he has adequate knowledge of anything; nevertheless he is certain to have, in many things, if not in all, such knowledge and such foundations that adequate knowledge could be deduced from them and perhaps already has been deduced. But who would support him?

Burman. V, 152.

109

L

LANGUAGE

There are only two things to be learned in any language, namely the signification of the words, and the grammar.

Letter to Mersenne, Nov. 20, 1629. I, 76.

❖   ❖   ❖

When one learns a language, he joins the letters or pronunciation of certain words, which are material things, with their significations, which are thoughts; in such a way that, when one later hears the same words again, one conceives the same things; and when one conceives the same things, one recalls the same words.

Letter to Chanut, Feb. 1, 1647. IV, 604.

❖   ❖   ❖

As for the signs that the dogs make with their tails, these are only the movements which accompany their feelings, and I believe that these must be distinguished carefully from language, which is the only certain sign of the thought which is hidden in the body.

Letter to More, Apr. 15, 1649. V, 344-345.

See *usage; words.*

LANGUAGE, NATURAL

The natural language is universal, as, when someone strikes us, we are obliged to cry out; if someone does something pleasant, to laugh.

Letter to Mersenne, Dec. 18, 1629. I, 102.

LANGUOR

Languor is a disposition to relax and to be without movement, which is sensed in all parts of the body.

Passions, II, 119. XI, 416.

111

And the passion which usually causes that affect [languor] is love, joined to the desire for something, the acquisition of which is not imagined as possible for the present time.

Passions, II, 120. XI, 417.

LAUGHTER

Laughter consists in the fact that the blood which comes from the right chamber of the heart by the arterial vein, inflates the lungs suddenly and repeatedly, so that the air which they contain is forced to come impetuously out of them through the windpipe, where it forms an inarticulate and striking voice.

Passions, II, 124. XI, 419.

❖ ❖ ❖

Although it seems that laughter is one of the principal signs of joy, nevertheless joy cannot cause laughter except when it is only mediocre, and when there is some wonder or hate mixed with it. For one finds by experience that when he is extraordinarily joyous, the subject of that joy never makes one break out in laughter.

Passions, II, 125. XI, 420.

LAWS

I have noticed certain laws, which God has so established in nature, and of which he has imprinted such notions in our souls, that after having reflected upon them sufficiently, we could not doubt that they are exactly observed in everything which is or which is done in the world.

Discourse, V. VI, 41.

❖ ❖ ❖

The common laws of society, which all tend to encourage us to do good to one another, or at least not to do bad, seem to me to be so well established that anyone who follows them openly, without any dissimulation or artifice, leads a life which is much happier and more assured than those who search for their own benefit by other ways.

Letter to Elisabeth, Jan., 1646. IV, 357.

LAWS OF NATURE

It may be believed, without denying the miracle of creation, that [God], having established the laws of nature, coordinated them in such a way that they act in a regular fashion, so that by these laws alone everything which is purely material could, given enough time, produce objects as we see them today.

Discourse, V. VI, 45.

❖   ❖   ❖

From the fact that God is not subject to change, and that he always acts in the same way, we can come to the knowledge of certain rules, which I call the laws of nature, and which are the secondary causes of various movements which we notice in all bodies.

Principles, II, 37. IX2, 84.

❖   ❖   ❖

The laws of nature are such that all bodies which move in rings must continually make some effort to move away from the centers about which they move.

Principles, III, 54. IX2, 130.

LEARNED MEN

Most of the questions about which learned men dispute are merely a matter of words.

Rules, XIII. X, 433.

LEARNING

We will never become mathematicians, even if we learn by heart all the demonstrations of other persons, if our mind is not at the same time capable of resolving any problem whatever; and we will never become philosophers, even if we have read all the reasonings of Plato and Aristotle, if we are incapable of making an assured judgment upon the subjects which are proposed to us; in such a case, we have not really learned mathematics or philosophy, it would seem, but history.

Rules, III, X, 367.

113

❖ ❖ ❖

I am accustomed to learning from everything in nature, even from the smallest ants and the tiniest grubs.

Letter to Beeckman, Oct. 17, 1630. I, 157-158.

❖ ❖ ❖

The little that I have learned until now is almost nothing, in comparison with what I do not know.

Discourse, VI. VI, 66.

LIFE

I am among those who love life the most.

Letter to Huygens, Oct. 10, 1642. III, 580.

❖ ❖ ❖

I do not say that any animal does not have life, which I say consists solely in the heat of the heart.

Letter to More, Feb. 5, 1649. V, 278.

❖ ❖ ❖

Warmth is the principle of life.

Passions, II, 107. XI, 407.

LIGHT

Proposing here to discuss the nature of light, I must first warn you that there is a difference between the sensation that we have, i.e., the idea that is formed in our imagination by the agency of our eyes, and what is in the objects which produce the sensation in us, i.e., what is in the flame or in the sun, which we call by the name "light."

The World, I. XI, 3.

❖ ❖ ❖

I know only two sorts of bodies in the world in which light is found, namely the stars and flame or fires.

The World, II. XI, 7.

❖ ❖ ❖

As for light, one can well conceive that the same movement, which is in the flame, suffices to make us see it.

The World, II. XI, 10.

◈　◈　◈

The principal properties of Light are: 1. that it extends around on all sides about a body which is called Luminous. 2. and at all distances. 3. and in an instant. 4. and ordinarily in straight lines, which should be taken as the rays of Light. 5. and that many of these rays, coming from various points, can be assembled in a single point. 6. or, coming from a single point, can be directed in various points. 7. or, coming from various points, and directed toward various points, can pass through a single point, without interfering with one another. 8. and that they can also sometimes interfere with one another, namely when their force is quite unequal, and when that of some is much greater than that of others. 9. and, lastly that they can be turned aside by reflection. 10. or by refraction. 11. and that their force can be augmented. 12. or diminished by the various dispositions or qualities of the matter which receives them.

The World, XIV. XI, 98.

◈　◈　◈

If it could be demonstrated [that the propagation of light is not instantaneous], then I would be prepared to confess that I knew nothing in philosophy.

Letter to Beeckman, Aug. 22, 1634. I, 308.

◈　◈　◈

I want you to think that light is nothing else, in the bodies that we call luminous, than a certain movement or a very prompt and lively action, which passes toward our eyes, by the agency of the air and of other transparent bodies.

Dioptrics, I. VI, 84.

◈　◈　◈

One should note that it is only those who can see during the shadows of the night, like cats, in whose eyes [light] is found.

Dioptrics, I. VI, 86.

❖   ❖   ❖

It is quite easy to believe that the action or inclination to move, which I have said ought to be taken for light, must follow in this the same laws as motion.

Dioptrics, I. VI, 89.

❖   ❖   ❖

Light is nothing other than a certain movement or an action received in a very fine material which fills the pores of other bodies.

Dioptrics, II. VI, 103.

❖   ❖   ❖

Light is nothing other than a movement, or an action which tends to cause some movement.

Dioptrics, V. VI, 129.

❖   ❖   ❖

I did not say that light was extended like a stick, but like the actions or movements which are transmitted by a stick.

Letter to Reneri, Apr.-May, 1638. II, 41.

❖   ❖   ❖

The way in which I conceive that the flame of a candle, or the light of a glowworm, etc., presses the subtle matter in a straight line toward our eyes, is the same as that in which I conceive that a stone, which is whirled about in a sling, presses against the middle of the sling, and draws out the cord in a straight line by the force only of its circular motion. The subtle matter which is around a candle or a glowworm moves in a circle about it, and tends [through centrifugal force] to move outward from the source and to leave an empty space, i.e., a space which could only be filled by matter coming from elsewhere.

Letter to Mersenne, Aug. 27, 1639. II, 572.

❖   ❖   ❖

I do not think that the light which strikes a body is anything other than the action, or the inclination to move toward it, that the particles of subtle matter have, which are impelled by the bodies that are called luminous.

Letter to Mersenne, Nov. 13, 1639. II, 618.

116

LIGHT, NATURAL

Disorderly studies and obscure meditations confuse the natural light and blind the mind; and those who walk habitually in the shadows weaken their vision so much that they later cannot bear the light of day.

Rules, IV. X, 371.

❖   ❖   ❖

The natural light, by itself, is sufficient for intuiting the truth which human reason obtains.

Rules, XIV. X, 440.

❖   ❖   ❖

God has given each of us a light for distinguishing the true from the false.

Discourse, III. VI, 27.

❖   ❖   ❖

I have as a rule for my [truths] only the natural light.

Letter to Mersenne, Oct. 16, 1639. II, 597.

❖   ❖   ❖

Since all men have the same natural light, it would seem that they should all have the same notions; but it is very different, in that there is almost no one who uses this light well.

Letter to Mersenne, Oct. 16, 1639. II, 598.

❖   ❖   ❖

When I say that it seems to me that that is taught to me by nature, I understand only by the word "nature" a certain inclination which leads me to believe that thing, and not a natural light which makes me know that it is true. But these two things differ greatly between them; for I cannot doubt anything that the natural light makes me see to be true, as it has just made me see that, from the fact that I doubted, I could conclude that I was. And I do not have any other faculty, or power, in me to distinguish the true from the false, which could teach me that what that light shows me as true is not true, and which I could trust more than I can trust it.

Meditations, III. IX, 30.

117

◈　◈　◈

[Things which pertain to the mind alone include], for example, the notion that I have of the truth that what has once been done cannot be undone, and an infinity of other similar things, which I know by the natural light, without the aid of the body.

Meditations, VI. IX, 65.

◈　◈　◈

We must note that the clarity of evidence by which our will can be excited to believe is of two sorts: one which comes from the natural light, and the other which comes from divine grace.

Replies, II. IX, 116.

◈　◈　◈

The faculty of knowing which [God] has given us, which we call natural light, never perceives any object which is not true insofar as it perceives it, i.e., insofar as it knows it clearly and distinctly; because we would have grounds for believing that God is a deceiver, if he had given it to us in such a way that we took the false for the true, when we used it correctly.

Principles, I, 30. IX2, 38.

◈　◈　◈

See *instincts; intuition.*

LIGHTNING

When the highest cloud falls only in pieces which follow one another, it causes almost nothing other than lightning and thunder; but when it falls in one piece and quite rapidly, it can also cause swirling winds and thunderbolts.

Meteorology, VII. VI, 318.

LIMITATION

Limitation is only a negation of a greater perfection, which negation is not due to cause; but only the limited thing itself [is due to a cause].

Replies, I. IX, 89.

LIQUID

A body is liquid when it is divided into many tiny particles which move separately in many different ways, and it is solid when all its particles touch one another, without acting so as to move apart from one another.

Principles, II, 54. IX 2, 94.

LIQUIDS

All hard bodies, composed of parts which are so equal or similar that they all can be agitated and separated equally easily from one another, become liquid when their particles are thus agitated and separated by the action of fire. For a body is liquid, simply from the fact that the particles of which it is composed move separately from one another.

◈　　◈　　◈

See *solid*.

LOGIC

As for logic, its syllogisms and most of its other instruction serve largely to explain the things that one knows to another person, or even, like the art of [Raymond] Lull, to speak, without judgment, about things that one does not know, rather than to learn anything.

Discourse, II. VI, 17.

◈　　◈　　◈

According to the laws of true logic, one ought never to ask of a thing, *if it is,* unless one knows first *what it is.*

Replies, I. IX, 85-86.

◈　　◈　　◈

All these consequences are derived without logic, without rules, without forms of argumentation, simply with the aid of the light of reason and good sense, which is less subject to deception when it acts alone and by itself than when it seeks anxiously to observe a thousand different rules that men have invented with artifice and laziness rather to corrupt good sense than to perfect it.

Search for Truth. X, 521.

119

◈　◈　◈

One ought to study Logic: not that of the School, because it is, properly speaking, only a Dialectic which teaches the means for making another person understand the things that one knows, or even to say without judgment many words concerning those things that one does not know, and thus logic corrupts good sense sooner than it increases it; but one ought to study the logic which teaches how to conduct his reason well, in order to discover the truths that he does not know; and because it depends heavily on practice, it is good for one to exercise over a long period of time, practicing the rules which apply to easy and simple questions, as do the rules of mathematics.

Principles, Preface. IX2, 13-14.

◈　◈　◈

The philosophers who attempt to explain, by the rules of their logic, things which are manifest of themselves, do nothing but obscure them.

Principles, I, 10. IX2, 29.

◈　◈　◈

See *dialectics; syllogisms.*

LOVE

There is a single active force in things: love, charity, harmony.

Cogitationes Privatae. X, 218.

◈　◈　◈

The true object of love is perfection.

Letter to Elisabeth, Sept. 15, 1645. IV, 291.

◈　◈　◈

[Purely intellectual or rational love] seems to me to be nothing other than that, when our soul perceives some good, either present or absent, which it judges to be suitable for it, it voluntarily joins itself to that good, that is, it considers itself with that good as a whole of which it is one part and the good is another part.

Letter to Chanut, Feb. 1, 1647. IV, 601.

120

❖　❖　❖

[Sensual or sensuous love] is nothing other than a confused thought excited in the soul by some movement of the nerves, which inclines it to the other, clearer thought of which rational love consists.

Letter to Chanut, Feb. 1, 1647. IV, 602-603.

❖　❖　❖

Two sorts of love are distinguished: one which is called love of benevolence, in which desire does not appear so much, and the other which is called love of concupiscence, which is only a very violent desire, founded upon a love which often is feeble.

Letter to Chanut, Feb. 1, 1647. IV, 606.

❖　❖　❖

When a thing is represented to us as good with respect to us, that is, as being suitable for us, that makes us have love for it; and when it is represented to us as evil or harmful, that excites us to hate.

Passions, II, 56. XI, 374.

❖　❖　❖

Love is an emotion of the soul, caused by the motion of the [animal] spirits, which incites it to join itself voluntarily to those objects which appear to it to be suitable.

Passions, II, 79. XI, 387.

❖　❖　❖

Two sorts of love are commonly distinguished, one of which is called benevolent love, that is, which incites one to wish good to that which he loves; the other is named concupiscent love, that is, which makes one desire the thing that he loves. But it seems to me that that distinction refers only to the effects of love, and not to its essence.

Passions, II, 81. XI, 388.

❖　❖　❖

That inclination or desire [for someone of the opposite sex] which is thus born of delight, is called by the name *love,* more frequently than the passion of love which has previously been

121

described. It also has the strangest effects, and it is this that serves as the principal matter for the novelists and poets.

Passions, II, 90. XI, 396.

❖   ❖   ❖

In love, when it is alone, that is, when it is not accompanied by any sort of joy, desire, or sadness, the pulse is regular, and much greater and stronger than usual; so that one senses a sweet warmth in the breast, and the digestion of food takes place quite promptly in the stomach: in such a way that this passion is useful for health.

Passions, II, 97. XI, 402.

LULL, RAYMOND

Three days ago, in an inn at Dordrecht, I met a wise man with whom I talked about the *Ars Parva* of Lull. He boasted that he could use the rules of that Art with such success that, he said, he could discourse for a full hour on any subject whatever; then, if someone asked him to speak for another hour on the same subject, he would be able to find completely different things to say, and so on, for another twenty hours.

To Beeckman, April 29, 1619. X, 164-65.

LUNGS

The principal purpose of the lungs consists only in the fact that, by means of the air of respiration, they cool and temper the blood which comes from the right chamber of the heart, before it enters the left; without this, the blood would be too rare and thin to serve as fuel for the fire in the heart. Their other use is to contain the air which serves to produce the voice.

Description of Human Body, II. XI, 236.

M

MACHINES

If there were machines which had the organs and the shape of a monkey, or of some other animal without reason, we would not have any way of telling that they were not of exactly the same nature as the animals.

Discourse, V. VI, 56.

❖   ❖   ❖

The invention of all these [simple] machines is founded upon a single principle, which is that the same force which can lift a weight, for example, of one hundred pounds to a height of two feet, can also lift one of 200 pounds to a height of one foot, or one of 400 to a height of a half foot, and similarly for the rest, depending upon how it is applied.

Treatise on Mechanics. I, 435-436.

❖   ❖   ❖

The [simple] machines which serve to apply a force which acts over a large space to a weight which is made to rise a small amount, are the pully, the inclined plain, the wedge, the wheel and axle, the vise, the lever; and several others.

Treatise on Mechanics. I, 436.

❖   ❖   ❖

In material things, all the causes of motion are the same as in machines made by artifice.

Letter to °°°, Mar., 1642(?). V, 544.

❖   ❖   ❖

I have described this earth, and generally all the visible world, as if it were only a machine in which there is nothing at all to consider other than the shapes and the motions of its parts; and nevertheless it is certain that our senses make it appear to us that there are many other things, namely, colors, odors, sounds, and all the other sensible qualities.

Principles, IV, 188. IX2, 310.

❖   ❖   ❖

We have not sufficiently accustomed ourselves to considering machines, and this is the origin of almost all the errors in philosophy.

Burman. V, 174.

❖   ❖   ❖

It is much more probable that earthworms, gnats, caterpillars and the rest of the animals move like machines, than that they have an immortal soul.

Letter to More, Feb. 5, 1649. V, 277.

MAGICAL WORDS

Men seem to be pronouncing magical words with an occult power when they say that *motion,* which is something that everyone knows perfectly well, is "the act of a being in potency, in so far as it is in potency." Who understands these words? Who is ignorant of what a motion is?

Rules, XII. X, 426.

MAGNANIMITY

I have called this virtue generosity, following the usage of our own language, rather than magnanimity following the usage of the School, where it is little known.

Passions, III, 161. XI, 453.

MAGNET

If there is some kind of entity in a magnet, which our understanding has never before perceived, there is no hope that we would ever be able to know it by reasoning; to know it we would have to have been given some new sense, or a divine revelation.

Rules, XIV. X, 439.

❖   ❖   ❖

So far I have attempted to explain the nature and all the principal properties of air, water, earth, and fire, because these are the bodies which are found most generally everywhere in this sublunary region that we inhabit, for which reason they are called the four elements; but there is still another body, namely the magnet, which could be said to be extended more widely than any one of these four, because the whole mass of the earth is a magnet, and because we cannot go anywhere where this characteristic is not found.

Principles, IV, 133. IX2, 271.

MAGNITUDE

No terms can be reduced to an equality except those which are capable of being more or less, and everything which is so reducible is included under the term *magnitude*.

Rules, XIV. X, 440.

MAJORITY VOTE

It would do no good to count votes, and to follow the opinion which has the majority: for, when we are concerned with a difficult question, it is more likely that few, rather than many, will have discovered the truth on this subject.

Rules, III. X, 367.

MALICE

The author would assert contradictory things if he said [that an evil demon was] very powerful and malicious, because supreme power and malice cannot exist together.

Burman. V, 151.

MAN

Although we can say that all created things are made for us, in the sense that we can derive some use from them, I nevertheless do not think that we are obliged to believe that man is the goal of creation.

Letter to Chanut, June 6, 1647. V, 53.

MASKS

Comedians, when they are called to the stage, put on a mask, so that the audience cannot see the blush on their cheeks. Like them, at the moment when I appear in the theater of the world where, until now, I have been only a spectator, I advance behind a mask.

Cogitationes Privatae. X, 213.

MATERIAL THING

There is no material thing of which the existence is assured.

Letter to °°°, May, 1637. I, 353.

MATERIAL THINGS

I have not proved the existence of material things from the fact that their ideas are in us, but from the fact that they are presented to us in such a way that we *know clearly* that they are not made by us, but that they come to us from elsewhere.

Letter to "Hyperaspistas," Aug., 1641. III, 428-429.

❖ ❖ ❖

[Material things] are perhaps not entirely such as we perceive them by the senses, because the perception of the senses is quite obscure and confused in many things; but at least it is necessary to say that all the things that I conceive clearly and distinctly, i.e., all the things, generally speaking, which are comprised in the object of speculative geometry, truly reappear there.

Meditations, VI. IX, 63.

MATERIALLY

See *formally*.

MATHEMATICS

Mathematics is full of very subtle inventions, and it is very useful, contenting the curious as well as facilitating every art and diminishing men's work.

Discourse, I. VI, 6.

❖ ❖ ❖

I liked mathematics best of all, because of the certainty and the evidence of its reasoning.

Discourse, I. VI, 7.

❖ ❖ ❖

Among all those who have previously sought truth in the sciences, only the mathematicians have been able to find *demonstrations,* that is, certain and evident reasons.

Discourse, II. VI, 19.

❖ ❖ ❖

I did not plan to try to learn all the particular sciences, which are commonly called mathematics.

Discourse, II. VI, 19.

❖　❖　❖

Mathematics habituates a person to recognizing the truth, because in mathematics are found right reasonings, which can hardly be found anywhere else. As a consequence, someone who has once accustomed his mind to mathematical reasonings will be able to search out the other truths, because the reasoning is the same everywhere.

Burman. V, 177.

❖　❖　❖

Mathematics habituates the mind to distinguishing which are the true and demonstrative reasonings, and which are the probable and false reasonings. For, in mathematics, anyone who relies solely on the probable is deceived and is led to the absurd.

Burman. V, 177.

❖　❖　❖

See *arithmetic*; *geometry*; *algebra*.

MATHEMATICS, GENERAL

I went from the particular study of arithmetic and geometry to an investigation of mathematics in general, asking first exactly what everyone understands by that word, and why, in addition to these two sciences, astronomy, music, optics, mechanics and many other sciences were also called parts of mathematics. It is not enough here simply to consider the etymology of the word; for the word "mathematics" signifies nothing other than "knowledge"; and every discipline might equally well be called mathematical, without limiting the term to geometry itself.

Rules, IV. X, 377.

MATHEMATICS, PURE

Even though all these things [techniques of mathematical induction] are so evident that they seem almost puerile, I understand, when I reflect attentively upon them, in what way they implicate all the questions which can be raised concerning proportions or the connections between things, and in what order they ought to be examined: this result alone summarizes what is essential in the whole science of pure mathematics.

Rules, VI. X, 384-385.

MATHEMATICS, UNIVERSAL

Although I often speak here of geometrical figures and numbers, because no other science gives examples which are as evident and as certain, whoever will attentively consider my thought will perceive easily that I am not thinking here about anything like ordinary mathematics, and that I am proposing a completely different discipline, of which the examples are the external, rather than the basic constituents. This science ought actually to contain the first rudiments of human reason, and to be capable of bringing forth the truths of any subject whatever; and, to speak frankly, I am persuaded that it is to be preferred to any other knowledge that we can attain through human means, because it is the source of all the others.

Rules, IV. X, 374.

❖ ❖ ❖

I asked myself why it happened that the ancient inventors of philosophy refused to admit anyone to the study of wisdom who was ignorant of mathematics, as though that discipline appeared to them to be the easiest of all, and the most necessary to form and prepare the mind to understand the other, more important sciences; and I began seriously to believe that they had known a type of mathematics which was completely different from the ordinary mathematics of our time.

Rules, IV. X, 376.

❖ ❖ ❖

Only those things, and all those things, in which order or measure are under consideration, are part of mathematics, whether one is seeking that measure in numbers, figures, the stars, sounds, or some other object; as a consequence there must be a general science which explains everything which

128

it is possible to investigate concerning order and measure, without assigning to it any particular subject whatever; and that science is called "universal mathematics," a name which is already ancient and part of accepted usage, rather than some name which is borrowed from another language [i.e., algebra]; for it contains everything in virtue of which one says of other sciences that they are parts of mathematics.

Rules, IV. X, 377-378.

MATTER

The idea that we have of body, or of matter in general, is included in that which we have of space, that is, that it is a thing which is long, wide and deep, just as the idea of a mountain is included in that of a valley.

Letter to Mersenne, Jan. 9, 1639. II, 482.

❖   ❖   ❖

Matter, or body in the general sense, does not consist in its being something hard, or heavy, or colored, or which touches our senses in some other way, but solely in the fact that it is a substance which is extended in length, width, and depth.

Principles, I, 4. IX2, 65.

❖   ❖   ❖

The earth and the skies are made of the same matter; and even if there were an infinity of worlds, they would be made only of that same matter.

Principles, II, 22. IX2, 75.

MECHANICS

I first considered in general all the clear and distinct notions which could be in our understanding concerning material things, and, not having found any others, except those which we have of shapes, sizes and motions, and the rules according to which these three things can be distinguished from one another, which rules are the principles of geometry and mechanics, I judged that it must necessarily be that all the knowledge that men could have about nature was derived from these alone; because all the other notions that we have of sensible things, being confused and obscure, cannot serve to give us the knowledge of anything outside ourselves, but rather can impede this knowledge.

Principles, IV, 203. IX2, 321.

❖ ❖ ❖

All the rules of mechanics belong to physics, in such a way that all the things which are artificial, are also natural.

Principles, IV, 203. IX2, 321-322.

MEDICINE
I am presently seeking a science of medicine which is founded upon infallible demonstrations.

Letter to Mersenne, Jan., 1630. I, 106.

MEMORY
He [Descartes] seemed to doubt that memory was distinguished from understanding and imagination. He did not believe that it could be extended or augmented, but only more or less filled up.

Studium Bonae Mentis. X, 200.

❖ ❖ ❖

We must correct for the weaknesses of our memory by using what might be called a continuous movement of thought.

Rules, VII. X, 387.

❖ ❖ ❖

The memory, on which depends the certainty of the conclusions which embrace more than we can grasp in a single act of intuition, though weak and liable to fail us, can be renewed and made stronger by a continuous and constantly repeated process of thought.

Rules, XI. X, 408.

❖ ❖ ❖

Memory — at least that which is corporeal and resembles the power which animals have to recall things — is nothing which is distinct from the imagination.

Rules, XII. X, 416.

❖   ❖   ❖

Among the innumerable dimensions which can be painted in our imagination, one ought not to contemplate more than two different ones in a single intuition, whether it is a case of visual or intellectual intuition; thus it is important to retain all the others, so that they are easily presented to us, each time that we have need of them; and it is for this purpose, it seems, that nature has instituted memory.

Rules, XVI. X, 454.

❖   ❖   ❖

One should never rely upon memory for anything which does not require continuous attention if it can be put on paper.

Rules, XVI. X, 458.

❖   ❖   ❖

These figures [imprinted in the brain] are not easily erased, but are retained there in such a way that, by means of them, ideas, which had previously been upon the [pineal] gland, can be formed there again long afterwards, without the presence of the objects to which they are connected. An this is what *memory* consists of.

Treatise on Man. XI, 178.

❖   ❖   ❖

The memory [is] what conserves the ideas.

Discourse, V. VI, 55.

❖   ❖   ❖

As for the species which are retained in memory, I do not imagine that they are anything other than like the folds which are retained in paper, after it has been folded once; and thus I believe that they are principally received in all the substance of the brain.

Letter to Meyssonnier, Jan. 29, 1640. III, 20.

❖   ❖   ❖

I believe that all the rest of the brain [other than the pineal gland] serves as the memory, principally its interior parts, and also that all the nerves and the muscles can serve as

131

memory; so that, for example, a lute player has part of his memory in his hands.

Letter to Mersenne, Apr. 1, 1640. III, 48.

❖ ❖ ❖

Besides that memory which depends upon the body, I recognize still another, completely intellectual, which depends only on the soul.

Letter to Mersenne, Apr. 1, 1640. III, 48.

❖ ❖ ❖

There is no doubt that the folds of the memory interfere with one another, and that there cannot be an infinity of such folds in the brain; but that does not prevent there being a great number of them; and the intellectual memory has its own species, which depend in no way upon these folds, of which I do not judge that the number must be very great.

Letter to Mersenne, June 11, 1640. III, 84-85.

❖ ❖ ❖

Besides the corporeal memory, the impressions of which can be explained by the folds of the brain, I judge that there is still another sort of memory in our understanding, which is completely spiritual, and which is not found in beasts; and that it is principally this memory that we use.

Letter to Mersenne, Aug. 6, 1640. III, 143.

❖ ❖ ❖

By the motion of the particles of the brain, a trace [*vestigium*] is made, upon which memory depends.

Letter to "Hyperaspistas," Aug., 1641. III, 425.

❖ ❖ ❖

As for [the memory] of things which are purely intellectual, properly speaking one has no memory [*recordatio*]; and one thinks of them as well when they are presented to the mind for the first time, as he does the second time, although perhaps they are customarily joined and quasi-attached to certain names which, being corporeal, make us also remember them.

Letter to "Hyperaspistas," Aug., 1641. III, 425.

132

◈　　◈　　◈

We shall someday find [the souls of friends who have died], even with recollection of the past; for I recognize in us an intellectual memory, which is assuredly independent of the body.

Letter to Huygens, Oct. 10, 1642. III, 580.

◈　　◈　　◈

As for memory, I believe that that of material things depends upon vestiges which remain in the brain, after some image has been imprinted there; and that that of intellectual things depends upon some other vestiges, which remain in the thought itself.

Letter to Mesland, May 2, 1644(?). IV, 114.

◈　　◈　　◈

About memory I can say nothing; everyone can find out for himself whether he has a good memory; if he has doubts, he ought to take notes or use similar helps.

Burman. V, 148.

◈　　◈　　◈

[Animals] have memory, like us, of material things; but they do not have thought or mind.

Generatio Animalium. XI, 519.

MEMORY, INTELLECTUAL

The intellectual memory is more of universal things than of singular things, and it is for this reason that we cannot recall all of our singular actions.

Burman. V, 150.

◈　　◈　　◈

[Recall] depends upon some reflection of the understanding, or intellectual memory.

Letter to Arnauld, June-July, 1648. V, 193.

MERCURY

As for mercury, its particles are so large that, pressing too strongly upon one another, they do not permit the matter of the second element to pass on any side of them, but only the matter of the first element.

Principles, IV, 16. IX2, 207.

133

METAPHYSICS

Concerning the questions which pertain to metaphysics, the principal difficulty is to conceive the first notions clearly and distinctly.

Replies, II. IX, 122.

◈ ◈ ◈

The first part [of the true philosophy] is metaphysics, which contains the principles of knowledge, among which is the explanation of the principal attributes of God, of the immateriality of our souls, and of all the clear and simple notions which are in us.

Principles, Preface. IX2, 14.

METHOD

It would be better never to think of seeking after truth, concerning any subject whatever, than to do so without a method.

Rules, IV. X, 371.

◈ ◈ ◈

By *method* I mean rules which are certain and simple, by the exact observation of which one will be sure never to confuse an error with the truth, and, without uselessly wasting the forces of his mind, and continuously increasing his knowledge, to arrive at the true knowledge of everything that he can know.

Rules, IV. X, 371-372.

◈ ◈ ◈

All method consists of the ordering and arrangement of those things toward which the mind turns, in order to discover some truth there. And we observe this order faithfully if we reduce by degrees those propositions which are complex and obscure to simpler propositions, and then, beginning with the intuition of the simplest of all, we attempt to advance, by the same steps, from the intuition of the simplest things to the knowledge of all the others.

Rules, V. X, 379.

134

I did not plan to explain all of the Method [in the *Discourse on Method*], but simply to say something about it.

Letter to Huygens, Feb. 25, 1637.

◈   ◈   ◈

I have formed a method by which it seems to me that I have the means to augment my knowledge by degrees, and to raise it little by little to the highest point to which the mediocrity of my mind and the brief duration of my life will permit it to attain.

Discourse, I. VI, 3.

◈   ◈   ◈

In the end, the method which teaches one to follow the true order, and to enumerate exactly all the circumstances for which he is searching, contains everything that gives certainty to the rules of arithmetic.

Discourse, II. VI, 21.

◈   ◈   ◈

My intention was not to teach my whole Method in the discourse where I proposed it, but only to say enough about it so that the novel opinions, which appear in the *Dioptrics* and the *Meteorology,* would not be taken lightly, and would perhaps be thought worth the trouble of examining them.

Letter to Vatier, Feb. 22, 1638. I, 559.

◈   ◈   ◈

See *order.*

MIND

The mind need not be contained within any limits whatever.

Rules, I. X, 360.

◈   ◈   ◈

[The power of knowing], according to its various functions, is sometimes called pure understanding, sometimes imagination, sometimes memory, sometimes sensation; but, properly speaking, it is called mind when it forms new ideas in the imagination [*phantasia*], or when it applies itself to those which are already traced there.

Rules, XII. X, 416.

The mind, although really distinguished from the body, is nevertheless joined to it, and is touched by the traces [*vestigia*] which are imprinted in it.

Letter to "Hyperaspistas," Aug., 1641. III, 424.

◈   ◈   ◈

Precisely speaking, I am nothing other than a thing which thinks, that is, a mind, an understanding or a reason.

Meditations, II. IX, 21.

◈   ◈   ◈

There is nothing which is easier for me to know than my mind.

Meditations, II. IX, 26.

◈   ◈   ◈

There is a great difference between the mind and the body, in that the body, by nature, is always divisible, and the mind is entirely indivisible.

Meditations, VI. IX, 68.

◈   ◈   ◈

The mind does not receive impressions from all parts of the body immediately, but only from the brain, or perhaps even from one of its smallest parts [i.e., the pineal gland].

Meditations, VI. IX, 69.

◈   ◈   ◈

I conceive the mind as a complete thing, which doubts, understands, wills, etc., while I do not grant to it any of the things which are contained in the idea of body.

Replies, I. IX, 95.

◈   ◈   ◈

Everything which can think is mind or is called mind. But, because body and mind are really distinct, no body is mind.

Replies, II. IX, 104.

◈   ◈   ◈

The substance in which thought immediately resides is here called *mind* [*spiritus, esprit*]. This word is equivocal, in that one also attributes it to wind or to very subtle liquids; but I do not think that this is the most proper meaning.

Replies, II. IX, 125.

❖   ❖   ❖

There are other acts which we call *intellectual,* as understanding, willing, imagining, sensing, etc., all of which agree among themselves in that they cannot be without thought, or perception, or consciousness and cognition; and the substance in which they reside, we say is *a thinking thing,* or *a mind,* or whatever other name we want to call it.

Replies, III. IX, 137.

❖   ❖   ❖

Certainly, in the same way and with just as much reason as he [Hobbes] concludes that the mind is a motion, he could also conclude that the earth is the sky, or any other such thing that he wishes; because there are no other things in the world between which there is as little similarity as there is between motion and mind, which are two entirely different types.

Replies, III. IX, 139.

❖   ❖   ❖

Being intelligent, willing, doubting, etc., are the forms by means of which I know that substance which is called *mind*.

Replies, IV. IX, 173.

❖   ❖   ❖

I do not now conceive that the mind is extended in the body otherwise [than weight], when I conceive it to be completely contained in the whole, and to be completely contained in each part.

Replies, IV. IX, 240.

❖   ❖   ❖

No one before me, as far as I know, asserted that mind consisted in *one thing alone,* namely the faculty of thinking and the inward source [of thinking].

Notes against a Program, I. VIII 2, 347.

The mind can never exist without thought; it can certainly exist without this or that thought, but not without any thought, just as body cannot, even for a moment, exist without extension.

Burman. V, 150.

MIND AND BODY

For the fact that the mind, which is incorporeal, can make the body move, there is neither reasoning nor comparison derived from other things which could teach us; but experiences which are very certain and very evident make us recognize it every day.

Letter to Arnauld, July 29, 1648. V, 222.

MIRACLES

The Lord has performed three miracles: he has created things from nothing, free will, and the Man-God.

Cogitationes Privatae. X, 218.

◈   ◈   ◈

There is a part of mathematics which I call the science of miracles, because it teaches how to make use of air and light in such a way that by means of it, one can produce all the same illusions as magicians are said to produce with the aid of demons.

Letter to °°°, Sept., 1629(?). I, 21.

◈   ◈   ◈

We will add, if we may, to our suppositions, that God will not perform any miracles in the world.

The World, VII. XI, 48.

MIRRORS

As for mirrors, I don't know anything about them that you don't know better than I do.

Letter to Mersenne, Feb. 25, 1630. I, 120.

MISER

A miser is mocked when he is jealous of his treasure, that is, when he covets it with his eyes, and never wants to be far from it, for fear that he will be robbed; for money is not worth the trouble that it takes to guard it so carefully.

Passions, III, 169. XI, 458.

MOCKERY

When [a good or evil] is represented to us as pertaining to other men, we can judge them to be worthy or unworthy of it. And when we judge them worthy, that excites no other passion in us than joy, insofar as it is a good to us to see things happen as they ought to. But there is this difference, that the joy which comes from good is serious; while that which comes from evil is accompanied by laughter and mockery.

Passions, II, 62. XI, 376-377.

MODE

When I say *mode* here, I understand only what I elsewhere call attribute or quality. But when I consider that the substance is modified or diversified by it, I use the particular word mode (or aspect); and when that disposition or change can be given a name, I call *qualities* the various modes which make it such that it can be so called; and finally, when I think more generally that the modes or qualities are in a substance, without considering them otherwise than as dependencies of that substance, I call them *attributes*.

Principles, I, 56. IX2, 49.

❖   ❖   ❖

I distinguish lines from surfaces, and points from lines, as one mode from another mode; but I distinguish the body from the surfaces, lines, and points which modify it, as a substance from its modes.

Letter to Mesland, May 2, 1644(?). IV, 119.

❖   ❖   ❖

Though we can easily comprehend a substance apart from a mode, we cannot, conversely, clearly comprehend a mode unless at the same time we conceive the substance of which it is a mode.

Notes against a Program, II. VIII 2, 350.

The nature of a mode consists in this, that it can by no means be comprehended, except it involve in its own concept the concept of the thing of which it is a mode.

> Notes against a Program, V. VIII 2, 355.

❖ ❖ ❖

See *aspects; substances.*

MOON

From the fact that we see that the moon is lighted only on the side which faces the sun, we can believe that it has no light of its own, and that it reflects only the rays that it receives from the sun toward our eyes.

> Principles, III, 10. IX2, 107.

MOTION

It is not possible to conceive of motion which does not have any duration.

> Rules, XII. X, 421.

❖ ❖ ❖

The philosophers themselves admit that the nature of motion, in their view, is difficult to understand, and to make it somewhat more intelligible, they have no better way of explaining it more clearly than in these terms: *Motus est actus entis in potentia, prout in potentia est* [motion is the act of a being in potency, insofar as it is in potency], which, for me, are so obscure that I must leave them in their language, because I do not know how to interpret them.

> The World, VII. XI, 39.

❖ ❖ ❖

As for me, I know of no way of explaining motion which is easier to conceive than the lines of the Geometricians, who make bodies pass from one place to another and occupy successively all the spaces which are between those two.

> The World, VII. XI, 39-40.

❖ ❖ ❖

Every body which moves tends always to continue its motion in a straight line.

> Letter to Mersenne, Jan. 9, 1639, II, 486.

I hold that there is a certain quantity of motion in all
created matter, which neither increases nor decreases at any
time; and thus, when one body in fact moves another, it
loses as much of its motion as it gives to the other.

Letter to Debeaune, Apr. 30, 1639. II, 543.

◇   ◇   ◇

[One knows] motion, at least that which goes from one
place to another (for the philosophers, in claiming other
motions that this, do not know so easily its true nature).

Principles, I, 69. IX2, 57.

◇   ◇   ◇

Motion, as we ordinarily take it, is nothing other than the
action by which one body passes from one place into another.

Principles, II, 24. IX2, 24.

◇   ◇   ◇

Motion, in truth, we will say, in order to attribute a determinate nature to it, is *the transport of one part of matter, or
of a body, from the neighborhood of those which touch it immediately, and which we consider as at rest, into the neighborhood of some others.*

Principles, II, 25. IX2, 76.

◇   ◇   ◇

All that is real in the bodies which move, in virtue of which
we say that they move, is found in parallel fashion in those
which touch them, although we consider them at rest.

Principles, II, 30. IX2, 79.

◇   ◇   ◇

The transference that I have called motion is not a thing
of less being than the shape, that is, it is a mode in the body,
and the moving force can come from God who conserves as
much transference in matter as he put into it at the first
motion of creation.

Letter to More, Aug., 1649. V, 403-404.

◇   ◇   ◇

See *magical words.*

MOTION, STRAIGHT-LINE

Of all the motions, it is only the straight-line motion which is entirely simple, and of which the nature is wholly comprised in an instant.

The World, VII. XI, 44-45.

MUSIC

The object of music is sound. Its purpose is to give pleasure, and to excite various passions in us.

Compendium Musicae. X, 89.

❖ ❖ ❖

The music of the ancients was more moving than ours, not because they were more learned, but because they were less.

Letter to Mersenne, Dec. 18, 1629. I, 101.

❖ ❖ ❖

Since music ought to imitate everything that happens in daily life, and since in quarrels and disorders many people often say different words at the same moment, why not permit music also to imitate that confusion?

Letter to Bannius, 1640.

N

NAMES

The collection which takes place in the reasoning process is not one of names, but rather of the things signified by the names.

Replies, III. IX, 139.

NATURAL

You ask me if I believe that water, in its natural state, is a liquid or a solid, to which I reply that I do not know anything which is violent [unnatural, extraordinary] in nature, except with respect to the human understanding, which gives the name violent to what is not according to its will, or according to which it judges that it ought to be; and it is equally natural for water to be frozen, when it is quite cold, as for it to be liquid, when it is less cold, because natural causes lead to either state.

Letter to Mersenne, Jan., (1638(?). I, 485.

❖   ❖   ❖

When a clock marks the hours by means of the wheels from which it is made, that is no less natural to it than it is to a tree to produce fruits.

Principles, IV, 203. IX2, 322.

NATURE

The great science of mechanics is nothing other than the order that God has imprinted upon the face of his work, which we commonly call *Nature*.

Letter to Villebressieu, Summer, 1631.

❖   ❖   ❖

By "Nature" I do not here understand some Goddess, or some other sort of imaginary power, but I use this word to signify Matter itself, insofar as I consider it with all the qualities that I have attributed to it, taken altogether, and under the condition that God continues to conserve it in the same way that he created it.

The World, VII. XI, 36-37.

❖   ❖   ❖

Nature always acts by the easiest and simplest means.

Treatise on Man. XI, 201.

❖   ❖   ❖

The multitude and the order of the nerves, veins, bones and other parts of an animal do not show that nature is not sufficient to form them, provided that one supposes that that nature acts always according to exact laws of mechanics, and that it is God who has imposed these laws.

Letter to Mersenne, Feb. 20, 1639. II, 525.

❖   ❖   ❖

Everything that nature teaches me contains some truth.

Meditations, VI. IX, 64.

❖   ❖   ❖

By nature, considered in general, I now understand nothing other than God himself, or rather the order and the disposition that God has established in created things.

Meditations, VI. IX, 64.

❖   ❖   ❖

By my nature in particular, I understand nothing other than the complex or the assemblage of all the things which God has given me.

Meditations, VI. IX, 64.

❖   ❖   ❖

Nature uses only means which are very simple.

Letter to Huygens, Oct. 10, 1642. III, 579.

❖   ❖   ❖

Nature is the same for all men.

Notes against a Program, IV. VIII 2, 354.

NATURE, INTELLIGENT

The intelligent nature is distinct from the corporeal nature.

Discourse, IV. VI, 35.

NATURES, PURE AND SIMPLE

There are very few pure and simple natures, of which we may have an immediate intuition, independently of anything else, either through direct experience or by means of some inner light.

Rules, VI. X, 383.

NATURES, TRUE AND IMMUTABLE

I find in myself an infinity of ideas of certain things, which cannot be regarded as purely nothing, even though they have no existence outside my thought, and which are not pretended by me, even though I am free to think of them or not to think of them; but they have their true and immutable natures. As, for example, when I imagine a triangle, even though there is, perhaps, no triangle anywhere in the world, outside my thought of such a figure, and even though there might never have been one, this figure nevertheless does not fail to have a true and immutable nature.

Meditations, V. IX, 51.

❖   ❖   ❖

Actually I recognize in many ways that the idea [of God] is nothing pretended or invented, depending simply on my thought, but that it is the image of a true and immutable nature.

Meditations, V. IX, 54.

❖   ❖   ❖

What we conceive clearly and distinctly to pertain to the nature, or to the essence, or to the immutable and true form of something, can be said or affirmed with truth of that thing.

Replies, I. IX, 91.

❖   ❖   ❖

The ideas which do not contain true and immutable natures, but only those which have been feigned or composed by the understanding, can be divided by the same understanding, not only by an abstraction or restriction of thought, but by a clear and distinct operation; so that the things that the

145

understanding cannot divide in this way have doubtless not
been made or composed by it.

Replies, I. IX, 92.

❖   ❖   ❖

See *essence.*

NAVIGATION

While I was leaving Middelburg, I thought about your art
of Navigation. And I really made a discovery: whatever the
location on the earth to which I might be carried, even if the
trip were made while I was asleep, and even if I did not know
the duration of it, I could know, solely by the inspection of
the stars, how many degrees to the east or west I was from
some known place.

To Beeckman, Mar. 26, 1619. X, 159.

NECESSARY

Although God has willed that some truths are necessary,
this is not to say that he has willed them necessarily; for it
is quite another thing to will that they be necessary, and to
will necessarily, or to be necessitated to will it.

Letter to Mesland, May 2, 1644(?). IV, 118.

NECESSITY

See *providence.*

NERVES

It is by the intermediary of the nerves that the impressions,
which objects make in the exterior members, travel to the
soul in the brain.

Dioptrics, IV. VI, 109.

❖   ❖   ❖

The nerves do not serve only to give sensation to parts of
the body, but also to move them.

Dioptrics, IV. VI, 110.

❖   ❖   ❖

The nerves are like tiny threads, or like tiny tubes, which
all come from the brain, and contain, as does the brain, a
certain air or very fine wind, which is called the animal spirits.

Passions, I, 7. XI, 332.

NON-BEING

Let us never forget that non-being, or that which does not exist, has no true attribute, and that one cannot conceive *the part, the whole, the subject, the adjunct,* etc., in it in any fashion.

Letter to More, Apr. 15, 1649. V, 344.

NOTHING

Nothing cannot produce anything.

Meditations, III. IX, 32.

❖　❖　❖

Not only is there a real and positive idea of God present to my thought, or rather of a supremely perfect being, but also, so to speak, a certain negative idea of nothing, that is, of what is infinitely distant from any sort of perfection; and I am like a mean between God and nothing, that is, placed between sovereign being and non-being.

Meditations, IV. IX, 43.

❖　❖　❖

Nothing, nor any perfection of a thing which actually exists, can have *Nothing,* or a non-existent thing, for the cause of its existence.

Replies, II. IX, 127.

❖　❖　❖

In metaphysics, *nothing* is comprehended on the basis of [our comprehension of] being.

Burman. V, 153.

❖　❖　❖

The difficulty that there is in knowing the impossibility of the void seems to come principally from the fact that we do not consider the fact that nothing cannot have any properties.

Letter to Arnauld, July 29, 1648. V, 223.

NUMBER

Those who attribute astonishing and mysterious properties to numbers would not have so much faith in these superstitions if they did not imagine that numbers were something distinct from the things which are numbered.

Rules, XIV. X, 445-446.

◇　◇　◇

The number that we consider in general, without reflecting upon any created thing, is nothing, outside of our thought, any more than all the other general ideas, which in the Schools are comprehended under the name universals.

Principles, I, 58. IX2, 50.

◇　◇　◇

When we see two stones, and when, without otherwise thinking about their nature, we notice only that there are two of them, we form in us the idea of a certain number which we name the number two. If, seeing later two birds or two trees, we notice again without thinking about their nature, that there are two of them, we again take up in this way the same idea that we had previously formed, and make it universal, and the number also to which we give a universal name, the number two.

Principles, I, 59. IX2, 50.

◇　◇　◇

See *size*.

O

OBJECTIVE BEING

That type of being [objective being of ideas] is certainly much more imperfect than that by which things exist outside our understanding; but still it is not a pure nothing.

Replies, I. IX, 82.

OBJECTIVE REALITY

It is quite difficult to understand how the idea of a supremely perfect being, which is found in us, contains so much objective reality, i.e., participates by representation in so many degrees of being and perfection, that it must necessarily come from a supremely perfect cause.

Meditations, Summary, IX, 11.

❖ ❖ ❖

By the *objective reality of an idea,* I understand the entity or being of the thing represented by the idea, insofar as that entity is in the idea; and in the same way, one can speak of an objective perfection, an objective artifice, etc. For everything that we conceive as being in the objects of ideas, all of that is objectively, or by representation, in the ideas themselves.

Replies, II. IX, 124.

OBJECTIVELY

To be objectively signifies nothing other than to be in the understanding in the manner in which objects are customarily there.

Replies, I. IX, 82.

OBSCURE

No conception is called obscure or confused, except because there is something contained in it which is not known.

Replies, II. IX, 115.

149

OBSERVATION

Observation, if it takes place through the medium of sight, can of its own proper power present nothing to the mind beyond pictures, and pictures consisting only of a permutation of corporeal movements.

Notes against a Program, XIV. VIII 2, 360.

ODOR

The sense of *odor* depends also upon many tiny threads, which come from the base of the brain toward the nose, below two small completely hollow particles, which the anatomists have compared to the ends of the breasts of a woman, and which differ in no way from the nerves which serve for touch and for taste, except that they do not come beyond the concavity of the head which contains the total brain, and that they can be moved by earthly particles which are still smaller than those which move the nerves of the tongue, partly because they are more immediately touched by the objects which move them.

Treatise on Man. XI, 147-148.

❖   ❖   ❖

The third [external sense] is odor, which has as its organ two nerves, which seem to be only parts of the brain which come forward toward the nose, because they do not go outside the skull; and as its object the tiny particles of terrestrial bodies which, when they are separated from one another, fly through the air; not all particles at random, but only those which are fine enough and penetrating enough to enter through the pores of the bone which is called spongy, when they are drawn in by the air of respiration, and move the tips of these nerves: and this motion takes place in as many different ways as there are different odors which we sense.

Principles, IV, 193. IX2, 313.

OLD AGE

Because, to the extent that one grows older, the tiny threads that compose the solid parts [of the body] grow tighter and attach themselves more and more to one another, they come at last to such a degree of hardness that the body entirely stops growing, and in addition it cannot even nourish itself;

150

with the result that it often comes to such a disproportion between the solid and fluid parts that old age alone brings an end to life.

Description of Human Body, III. XI, 250.

ORDER

Those who examine difficult questions out of their proper order seem to me to be like those who want to jump, in a single leap, from the ground to the roof of some house, paying no attention to the ladders that are provided for this purpose, or else not noticing then.

Rules, V. X, 380.

❖ ❖ ❖

So that the simplest things can be distinguished from the involved, and so that they can be investigated in order, we must form a series of terms in which we have deduced certain truths directly from others, and we must identify the simplest, and find out how far the other terms are from it.

Rules, VI. X, 381.

❖ ❖ ❖

In everything that I write, I do not follow the order of the material, but solely that of the reasons; that is, I do not attempt to say in one place everything that pertains to a given subject, because it would be impossible for me to prove it adequately, since there are some reasons which ought to be derived much later than others; but in reasoning in order *a facilioribus ad difficiliora* [beginning with the easiest and going on to the more difficult], I deduce whatever I can, now for one subject, now for another; which is, in my opinion, the true path for finding and explaining the truth.

Letter to Mersenne, Dec. 24 ,1640(?). III, 266.

❖ ❖ ❖

Order consists only in this, that the things which are proposed first ought to be known without the aid of those which follow, and that the later ones ought to be arranged in such a way that they are demonstrated solely by what precedes them.

Replies, II. IX, 121.

❖   ❖   ❖

See *method*.

ORTHOGRAPHY

I do not have any plans for reforming French orthography, nor would I want to advise anyone to learn it from a book printed at Leyden; but if I have to give my opinion here, I believe that if one followed pronunciation exactly, that would make it much easier for foreigners to learn our language, since the ambiguity of various equivocal expressions would not cause trouble for them or for us.

Letter to Reneri, Apr.-May, 1638. II, 46.

P

PAIN

If the tiny threads, which compose the marrow of the nerves, are pulled with so much force that they break, and are separated from the particles to which they have been joined, so that the structure of the whole machine [the body] is somehow weakened: the movement that they cause in the brain will give occasion to the soul, taking note of its location, to have the sensation of *pain*.

Treatise on Man. XI, 143-144.

❖   ❖   ❖

I do not explain the sensation of pain without the soul; for, according to me, pain is only in the understanding; but I explain all the external motions which accompany this sensation in us, and which are the only things found in beasts, who do not feel pain, properly speaking.

Letter to Mersenne, June 11, 1640. III, 85.

❖   ❖   ❖

There is no reason which obliges us to believe that the pain which we sense, for example, in the foot is anything outside our thought which is in our foot.

Principles, I, 67. IX2, 56.

❖   ❖   ❖

If the same action [which causes pleasure] has a little more force, such that it causes harm to our body in some way, this gives to our soul the sensation of pain. And thus it is seen how the pleasure of the body and pain are entirely contrary sensations in the soul, even though often the one follows the other, and even though their causes are almost similar.

Principles, IV, 191. IX2, 313.

❖   ❖   ❖

See *pleasure*.

153

PANIC TERROR

[Panic Terror:] I, the daughter of the night, cold, pale and trembling, when I wish to terrify a million warriors, who will trample their laurels under their feet, need only a monster, a dream, or a faint shadow, which I send into their brains. And they tremble like calves, they flee, they turn pale, and often they throw themselves into more fearful evils than those that they tried to avoid.

Birth of Peace, III.

PARTICLES

It is not in the flame alone that there is a quantity of small particles which do not cease to move; but there are particles in all other bodies, even though their actions are not so violent, which, because of their smallness, cannot be perceived by any of our senses.

The World, III. XI, 11.

◈   ◈   ◈

Each body can be divided into extremely small particles. I do not want to determine whether their number is infinite or not; but at least it is certain that, with respect to our knowledge, it is indefinitely large, and that we can suppose that there are many millions in the smallest grain of sand which can be perceived by our eyes.

The World, III. XI, 12.

◈   ◈   ◈

I suppose first that the water, the earth, the air, and all other such bodies which surround us are composed of many tiny particles of various shapes and sizes, which are never so well arranged nor so perfectly joined together that there are not many intervals around them; and that these intervals are not empty, but filled with the very subtle matter by means of which, as I have said, the action of light is communicated.

Meteorology, I. VI, 233.

◈   ◈   ◈

All bodies are composed of particles, which is something

154

that can be seen with the naked eye in many things, and
which can be proved by an infinity of reasons in others.

Letter to Morin, July 13, 1638. II, 200.

❖　❖　❖

I do not propose any other difference between the particles
of earthly bodies and those of subtle matter than as between
rocks and the dust which comes from these rocks when one
of them is rubbed against the other.

Letter to Mersenne, Jan. 9, 1639. II, 485.

PASSION

The number of simple and primitive [passions] is not very
great. For, reviewing all those that I have enumerated, one
can easily notice that there are only six which are primitive,
namely, wonder, love, hate, desire, joy, and sadness; and that
all the others are composed of some of these six, or are species
of these.

Passions, II, 69. XI, 380.

❖　❖　❖

The principal seat of the passions, insofar as they concern
the body, is in the heart, because it is the heart which is most
altered by them; but their place is in the brain, insofar as
they affect the soul, because the soul cannot be immediately
acted upon except by the brain.

Letter to Regius, May, 1641. III, 373.

❖　❖　❖

Other motions of the same nerves make it [the soul] sense
other passions [than joy and sadness], such as those of love,
hate, fear, anger, etc., insofar as these are sensations or passions of the soul; that is, insofar as these are confused thoughts
which the soul does not have of itself, but from the fact that
it is tightly united to the body, and thus receives the impression of the movements which take place in it; for there is a
great difference between these passions and the knowledge or
distinct thoughts which we have of what is loved, or hated,
or feared, etc., even though these are often found together.

Principles, IV, 190. IX 2, 312.

In general, all the thoughts which are excited in the soul without the concurrence of the will, and, as a consequence, without any action which comes from the will, solely by means of the impressions which are in the brain, can be called passions, for everything which is not an action is a passion. But this name is ordinarily restricted to the thoughts which are caused by some particular agitation of the [animal] spirits.

Letter to Elisabeth, Oct. 6, 1645. IV, 310.

◈   ◈   ◈

As for the movements of our passions, even though they are accompanied by our thought, because we do have the faculty of thinking, it is nevertheless very evident that they do not depend upon it, because they often occur in spite of us.

Letter to Newcastle, Nov. 23, 1646. IV, 573-574.

◈   ◈   ◈

All the movements of our [bodily] members which accompany our passions or affections are produced, according to me, not by our soul, but solely by the mechanism of our body.

Letter to More, Apr. 15, 1649. V, 344.

◈   ◈   ◈

The philosophy that I cultivate is not so barbarous or fierce that it rejects the enjoyment of the passions; on the contrary, it is in them alone that I place all the sweetness and happiness of this life.

Letter to Newcastle, Mar. or Apr., 1648. V, 135.

◈   ◈   ◈

Everything that is done or which happens, is generally called by the philosophers a *passion* with regard to the subject to which it happens, and an *action* with regard to what makes it happen. As a result, even though the agent and the patient are often quite different, action and passion are nevertheless the same thing, which has two names, because of the two different subjects to which it can be referred.

Passions, I, 1. XI, 328.

◆ ◆ ◆

The last and most proximate cause of the soul is nothing other than the agitation with which the [animal] spirits move the tiny [pineal] gland which is at the center of the brain.

Passions, II, 51. XI, 371.

◆ ◆ ◆

The utility of all the passions consists only in the fact that they dispose the soul to wish the things which nature tells us to be useful, and to persist in that wish.

Passions, II, 52. XI, 372.

PASSIONS OF THE SOUL

After having considered the ways in which the passions of the soul differ from all its other thoughts, it seems to me that they can be defined in general: Perceptions, or sensations, or emotions of the soul, which are referred particularly to it, and which are caused, supported, and fortified by some movement of the [animal] spirits.

Passions, I, 27. XI, 349.

PEACE

[The Earth:] I am afraid that soon the world will perish or be lost and become a chaos, if the gods do not send peace to these lands.

Birth of Peace, X.

◆ ◆ ◆

See *war*.

PEOPLE

I am going to walk every day among the confusion of a great people, with as much freedom and repose as you would have in your back streets, and I do not consider the men that I see there any differently than I would the trees that are found in your forests, or the animals that graze there.

Letter to Balzac, May 5, 1631. I, 203.

PERCEPTION

The perception [of a piece of wax], or rather the action by which it is perceived, is not a vision, or touch, or imagina-

157

tion, and has never been, although it seemed so previously, but solely a scrutiny of the mind [*mentis inspectio*], which can be imperfect and confused, as it was previously, or clear and distinct, as it is at present, according to whether my attention is turned more or less to the things which are in it, and of which it is composed.

Meditations, II. IX, 24-25.

❖   ❖   ❖

The thought of each person, that is, the perception or knowledge that he has of a thing, ought to be for him the rule of truth concerning that thing, that is, all the judgments that he makes about it ought to conform to that perception to be valid; even concerning the truths of the faith, we ought to perceive some reason which persuades us that they have been revealed by God, before we determine to believe them; and although ignorant persons do well to follow the judgment of the more capable concerning things which are difficult to know, it is nevertheless necessary that it is their perception which teaches them that they are ignorant and that those whose judgments they wish to follow are perhaps not so ignorant; otherwise they would do ill to follow them, and they would act rather like automata or beasts than like men.

Letter to Clerselier. IX, 208.

❖   ❖   ❖

All the ways of thinking which we notice in ourselves can be referred back to general ways, one consisting in perception by the understanding, and the other in determining oneself by the will. Thus sensing, imagining and even conceiving purely intelligible things, are only different ways of perceiving; but desiring, having an aversion, assenting, denying, doubting, are different ways of willing.

Principles, I, 32. IX2, 39.

❖   ❖   ❖

My perception is the sole rule by which I ought to affirm or deny.

Letter to More, Apr. 15, 1649. V, 344.

158

◆　◆　◆

Our perceptions are of two sorts, some of which have the soul as cause, others the body. Those which have the soul as cause are the perceptions of the acts of our will, and of all the imaginations or other thoughts which depend upon them.

Passions, I, 19. XI, 343.

◆　◆　◆

Among the perceptions which are caused by the body, the greater number depend upon the nerves; but there are also some others which do not depend upon them, and which are called imaginations [i.e. dreams and reveries].

Passions, I, 21. XI, 344.

PERCEPTIONS

Those [perceptions] which we refer to external objects, that is, to objects of our senses, are caused (at least when our opinion is not false) by those objects, which, exciting some movements in the external sense organs, also excite movements in the brain, by means of the nerves; and these movements make the soul sense.

Passions, I, 23. XI, 346.

◆　◆　◆

The perceptions which we refer to our body, or to some of its parts, are those which we have of hunger, thirst, and our other natural appetites; to which can be added pain, warmth, and the other feelings which we sense as in our members, and not as in external objects.

Passions, I, 24. XI, 346-347.

◆　◆　◆

The perceptions which we refer exclusively to the soul are those whose effects are sensed as in the soul itself, and whose proximate cause is not generally known, to which they could be referred. Such are the sensations of joy, anger, and other similar sensations, which are sometimes excited in us by the objects which move our nerves, and sometimes also by other causes.

Passions, I, 25. XI, 347.

[The passions] can be called perceptions, when this word is used in a general sense to signify all the thoughts which are not actions of the soul, or acts of will; but not when the word perception is used only to signify evident knowledge.

Passions, I, 28. XI, 349.

PERFECTION

I could not actually conceive an imperfect triangle, if there were not in me the idea of a perfect triangle, of which it is the negation; and thus, seeing a triangle, I conceive the perfect triangle, then, by comparison with it, I notice that the triangle that I see is imperfect.

Burman. V, 162.

PERPETUAL MOTION

There is surely no doubt that perpetual motion, about which you write me, is impossible.

Letter to Mersenne, Aug. 27, 1639. II, 573.

PERSON

Even though each one of us is a person separate from others and, as a consequence, has interests distinct in some way from those of the rest of the world, one ought in any case to think that he could not subsist alone, and that he is, actually, one of the parts of the universe, and more particularly still one of the parts of this earth, one of the parts of this State, of this society, of this family, to which he is joined by his residence, by his oath, by his birth.

Letter to Elisabeth, Sept. 15, 1645. IV, 293.

PERSPECTIVE

Paintings in perspective show us how easy it is to be deceived.

Treatise on Man. XI, 162.

PERSUASION

I make a distinction between persuasion and science. *The first* is found in us when there is still some reason which could lead us to doubt; and *the second,* when the reason for believing is so strong that there is never any other reason present which is more powerful, and which is such at least that whose who do not know that there is a God could not have a belief like it.

Letter to Regius, May 24, 1640. III, 65.

PHILOSOPHER

No one could imagine anything so strange or unbelievable that it has not been said by some philosopher.

Discourse, II. VI, 16.

❖　❖　❖

There is nothing more praiseworthy for a philosopher than sincerely to admit his errors.

Letter to Regius, Jan., 1642(?). III, 492.

PHILOSOPHIZING

To live without philosophizing is really to have one's eyes closed without ever trying to open them.

Principles, Preface IX2, 3.

PHILOSOPHY

Philosophy gives one the means for speaking plausibly about everything, and making one admired by the least learned.

Discourse, I. VI, 6.

❖　❖　❖

I will say nothing about philosophy, except that, seeing that it has been cultivated over many centuries by the most excellent minds who have lived, and that nevertheless nothing at all has yet succeeded about which no one disputes, and as consequence which is doubtful, I did not have enough presumption to hope to find anything where others had failed.

Discourse, I. VI, 8.

❖　❖　❖

Instead of that speculative philosophy which is taught in the schools, one can find a practical philosophy, by which, knowing the force and actions of fire, water, air, stars, heavens and all the other bodies which surround us, as distinctly as we know the various occupations of our artisans, we would be able to apply them in the same way to all the uses to which they are proper and thus make ourselves like masters and possessors of nature.

Discourse, VI. VI, 61-62.

161

◈   ◈   ◈

If my philosophy seems to him [Fromondus] to be too gross, in that it considers shapes, sizes and movements, as does Mechanics, he is condemning just the thing that I think is most to be praised, and what I prefer in it above all other philosophies and take most pride in, which is to use a kind of philosophy where no reason is ever admitted which is not mathematical or evident, and in which the conclusions are all founded upon very certain experiments.

Letter to Plempius, Oct. 3, 1637. I, 420-421.

◈   ◈   ◈

In philosophy everyone believes that all its propositions are problematic, so that few persons devote themselves to the search for truth; and many people, who want to get a reputation for having a powerful mind, study nothing but how to combat arrogantly against the most obvious truths.

Meditations, Dedication. IX, 7.

◈   ◈   ◈

All of philosophy is like a tree, of which the roots are metaphysics, the trunk is physics, and the branches that come from this trunk are all the other sciences, which can be reduced to three principal ones, namely medicine, mechanics, and ethics, intending by this the highest and more perfect ethics, which, presupposing a complete knowledge of the other sciences, is the highest degree of wisdom.

Principles, Preface. IX2, 14.

PHILOSOPHY, TRUE

The invention of a language depends upon the true philosophy, for it would otherwise be impossible to enumerate all the thoughts of men, and place them in order, or even to distinguish those which are clear and simple, which is, I think, the most important secret in acquiring true knowledge.

Letter to Mersenne, Nov. 20, 1629. I, 81.

PHYSICS

The goal of true physics should be usefulness to human society and lightening the burden of human labor.

Rules, XIII (quoted in Port Royal Logic)

◇ ◇ ◇

Rather than explaining only one phenomenon, I have resolved to explain all the phenomena of nature, that is, all of physics.

Letter to Mersenne, Nov. 13, 1629. I, 70.

◇ ◇ ◇

In physics, I attempt to treat only that which is universal and which everyone can experience.

Letter to Mersenne, Dec. 18, 1629. I, 85.

◇ ◇ ◇

All my physics is nothing other than mechanics.

Letter to Debeaune, Apr. 30, 1639. II, 542.

◇ ◇ ◇

Concerning physics, I would believe that I knew nothing about it if I knew only how to say how things could be, without demonstrating that they could not be otherwise.

Letter to Mersenne, Mar. 11, 1640. III, 39.

◇ ◇ ◇

The second [branch of philosophy] is Physics, in which, after having found the true principles of material things, one examines in general how the universe is composed, then in particular the nature of this earth and of all the bodies which are found most commonly around it, such as air, water, fire, the magnet and other minerals.

Principles, Preface. IX 2, 14.

PIETY

No men more easily attain a great reputation for piety than the superstitious and the hypocritical.

Principles, Dedication. IX, 22.

PINEAL GLAND

My opinion is that the [pineal] gland is the principal seat of the soul, and the place where all our thoughts take place.

Letter to Meyssonnier, Jan. 29, 1640. III, 19.

◇ ◇ ◇

The part of the body in which the soul most immediately exercises its functions is not the heart; nor is it the brain, but

163

solely the most internal of its parts, which is a certain very small gland, [i.e., the pineal gland], situated in the midst of the substance of the brain, and suspended above the passage by which the [animal] spirits from its anterior cavities communicate with those of the posterior, in such a way that the slightest movements which it makes can greatly change the course of these spirits; and, reciprocally, that the slightest changes that occur in the flow of the spirits can greatly change the movements of that gland.

Passions, I, 31. XI, 352.

❖   ❖   ❖

And every action of the soul consists in that, by the sole fact that it wills something, it makes the little [pineal] gland, to which it is so tightly joined, move in the fashion which is required to produce the effect which corresponds to that act of the will.

Passions, I, 41. XI, 360.

❖   ❖   ❖

See *sense, common.*

PITY

Pity is a species of sadness, mixed with love or good will toward those whom we see suffering from some evil, which we believe that they do not deserve.

Passions, III, 185. XI, 469.

❖   ❖   ❖

Those who feel quite weak and much subject to the adversities of fortune seem to be more inclined to this passion than others, because they think of the evil that happens to others as happening to themselves; and thus they are moved to pity, rather by the love that they feel for themselves than by that which they have for others.

Passions, III, 186. XI, 469.

❖   ❖   ❖

But it is only the evil and envious spirits who naturally hate all men, or rather those who are so brutal and so blinded by good fortune, or so desperate because of bad fortune, that they do not think that any further evil can happen to them, who are insensible to pity.

Passions, III, 188. XI, 470-471.

PLACE

When learned men define *place* as "the surface of the surrounding body," they do not really represent anything to themselves which is false; they only abuse the term "place," which in common usage designates that simple and self-evident nature by virtue of which it is said that an object is found here or there; a nature which consists entirely in a certain relation of the thing which is said to be found in such a place to the regions of the surrounding space.

Rules, XIII. X, 433.

❖　❖　❖

The words place and space do not signify anything which actually differs from the body which is said to be in some place, and they simply denote for us its size, its shape, and how it is situated among the other bodies.

Principles, II, 13. IX2, 69-70.

❖　❖　❖

We cannot find in all the universe any point which is truly immobile (which we will later demonstrate), and we conclude that there is no place for anything in the world which is firm and unmoving, except insofar as we stop it in our thought.

Principles, II, 13. IX2, 70.

PLANETS

Those particles of matter which swirl toward the center of a given Sky are here to be regarded as Planets.

The World, IX. XI, 60.

❖　❖　❖

There is still another difference among the stars, which consists in the fact that some keep the same order among themselves, and are always found equally distant from one another, which is the reason that they are called fixed; and others continually change their relative position, which is the reason that they are called planets or wandering stars.

Principles, III, 14. IX2, 108.

PLAUSIBILITY

If they want to know how to talk about everything and get

165

the reputation of being learned, they will succeed at it most easily if they content themselves with plausibility, which can be found without great effort in all sorts of subjects, rather than seeking for the truth, which is not found except little by little in a few subjects, and which, when it is a matter of speaking about other subjects, obliges one to confess frankly that he does not know them.

Discourse, VI. VI, 71.

PLAUSIBLE

I believe that what is merely plausible is almost like what is false.

Letter to Mersenne, Oct. 5, 1637. I, 450.

PLEASURE

When the nerves are moved a little more strongly than usual, and in such a manner that our body is not hurt in any way, this causes the soul to sense the pleasurable sensation which is also a confused thought; and this thought is naturally agreeable to it, so much so that it bears witness to the strength of the body to which the soul is joined, in that it can be acted upon by whatever causes the sensation without being harmed.

Principles, IV, 191. IX2, 313.

PLEASURES

There are two sorts of pleasures: those which belong to the mind alone, and those which belong to man, that is, to the mind insofar as it is united to a body.

Letter to Elisabeth, Sept. 1, 1645. IV, 284.

POETS

It seems astonishing that profound thoughts are found more often in the writings of poets than in those of philosophers. The reason for it is that the poets have written in enthusiasm and with the power of the imagination. We have within us certain seeds of knowledge, as a flint has seeds of fire; philosophers extract them through reason; poets snatch them out through imagination; they burn all the more brilliantly then.

Cogitationes Privatae. X, 217.

PORES

All terrestrial bodies have many pores, through which the smallest [particles] can pass.

Meteorology, I. VI, 235.

POSITION

As for position, i.e., the side toward which each part of the object is placed, we do not perceive it by means of our eyes otherwise than by means of our hands; and knowledge of it does not depend upon any image, nor upon any action which comes from the object, but simply from the position of the tiny particles of the brain from which the nerves originate.

Dioptrics, VI. VI, 134.

POSSIBLE

Either you understand by the word *possible* what is ordinarily understood [i.e.], all that is not repugnant to human thought, in which sense it is manifest that the nature of God is possible, in the way in which I have described it, because I have not supposed anything in it except what we conceive clearly and distinctly ought to belong to him, and thus I have supposed nothing which is repugnant to human thought or concept; or you are claiming some other possibility, on the part of the object itself, which, if it is not consistent with the first definition, can never be known by human understanding.

Replies, II. IX, 118.

POVERTY

[Peasants, ruined by the war:] Our distress is great; we have neither horses nor cattle with which to work; neither butter nor chickens nor eggs to take to sell beyond the village. Thus everyone knows that poverty teaches us idleness.

Birth of Peace, IX.

PRAISE

It is as useful to be blamed by one's friends as to be praised by one's enemies. From strangers, we expect praise; from our friends, the truth.

Cogitationes Privatae. X, 217.

❖   ❖   ❖

I am not insensitive to praise, but I believe that it is a greater good to enjoy tranquility in my life, and an honest leisure, than to acquire much renown.

Letter to Beeckman, Oct. 17, 1630. I, 164.

PRAYERS

Theology does not admit change [in God's will]; and when it obliges us to pray to God, it is not to teach him what we have need of, nor to attempt to obtain from him some change in the order which has been established from all eternity by his providence: either one of these aims would be blameworthy; but it is solely to obtain what he has wished from all eternity for us to obtain by our prayers.

Letter to Elisabeth, Oct. 6, 1645. IV, 316.

PREJUDICE

The word prejudice does not extend to all the notions which are in our mind, which I admit that it is impossible to get rid of, but only to all the opinions which the judgments that we have previously made have left among our beliefs.

Letter to Clerselier. IX, 204.

❖   ❖   ❖

To get rid of every sort of prejudice, nothing else is necessary than to resolve to affirm or deny none of the things that one had affirmed or denied previously.

Letter to Clerselier. IX, 204.

❖   ❖   ❖

Although one could give the name [prejudice] to this proposition [that I think, therefore I am], when one utters it without attention, and when one believes that it is true only because one remembers having judged it thus previously, one cannot say nevertheless that it is a prejudice when one examines it, because it appears so evident to the understanding that it cannot be prevented from believing it, even though it is, perhaps, the first time in one's life that he has thought of it, and as a consequence it is no prejudice.

Letter to Clerselier. IX, 205.

We have been so strongly predisposed by a thousand prejudices that, by the time we are capable of using our reason properly, we have already received them as beliefs; and instead of thinking that we had made these judgments at a time when we were not capable of judging properly, and as a consequence that they were more likely to be false than true, we have received them as though they were as certain as if we had had distinct knowlege by means of our senses, and have no more doubted them than we would if they were common notions.

Principles I, 71. IX 2, 59.

PRESSURE

The pressure [of the particles of light] can take place without motion: for example, if we press upon a piece of iron or wood with our hands from both sides, in such a way that no motion is produced, because the pressure is equal on both sides, and the resistance also is equal.

Burman. V, 172.

PRESUMPTION

If one imagines that beyond the skies there is nothing but imaginary spaces, and that all these heavens are made only for the service of the earth, and the earth for man, this makes one inclined to think that this earth is our principal residence, and this life our best; and that instead of knowing the perfections which are truly in us, one attributes to other creatures imperfections which they do not have, to elevate ourselves above them, and, entering into an impertinent presumption, one wishes to give advice to God, and take charge with him of the conduct of the world, which causes an infinity of vain anxieties and vexations.

Letter to Elisabeth, Sept. 15, 1645. IV, 292.

PRIDE

The good which is or which has been in us, when it is connected to the opinion that others can have, excites pride in us; and evil, shame.

Passions, II, 66. XI, 378.

169

Pride is always vicious, although it is all the more so as the cause for which one esteems himself is the less justified. And it is the least justified of all when one is prideful without any reason.

Passions, III, 157. XI, 448.

❖   ❖   ❖

What I here call by the name of pride is a species of joy, founded upon the love that one has for oneself, and which comes from the opinion or the hope that one has of being praised by some other persons.

Passions, III, 204. XI, 482.

PRIMITIVE NOTIONS

There are in us certain primitive notions, which are the originals, on the pattern of which we form all our other knowledge. And there are only a very few such notions; for, after the most general, of being, number, duration, etc., which apply to all that we can conceive, we have, for body in particular, only the notion of extension, from which follow those of shape and motion; and for the soul alone, we have only that of thought, in which are comprised the perceptions of the understanding and the inclinations of the will; finally, for the soul and the body together, we have only that of their union, upon which depends that of the force which the soul has of moving the body, and the body for acting upon the soul, causing its sensations and its passions.

Letter to Elisabeth, May 21, 1643. III, 665.

PRINCIPLES

I would not dare affirm that the things which I enunciate are the true principles of Nature, but I will say at least that when I take them as principles, I customarily satisfy myself about all the things that depend upon them.

Fragment 6, 1633-1635? IV, 686.

❖   ❖   ❖

I have always remained firm in the resolution which I made, to suppose no other principles than those which I have just used to demonstrate the existence of God and of the soul, and to accept nothing whatever as true, which does not seem to me to be clearer and more certain than the demonstrations of geometry previously appeared.

Discourse, V. VI, 41.

❖ ❖ ❖

I attempted in general to find the principles, or first causes, of everything that is, or which can be, in the world, considering nothing, to this effect, other than God alone, who has created the world, nor to derive them otherwise than from certain seeds of truth which are naturally in our souls.

Discourse, VI. VI, 63-64.

❖ ❖ ❖

Not admitting any principle which is not most manifest, and considering nothing other than sizes, shapes and motions, in the style of the mathematicians, I have insured myself against all the subterfuges of the philosophers, and the slightest error which slips into my principles can be easily perceived and refuted by a mathematical demonstration.

Letter to Plempius, Oct. 3, 1637. I, 410-411.

❖ ❖ ❖

The interconnection of my thoughts is such that I dare to hope that my principles will be found to be as well proved by the consequences that I have derived from them, when they have been studied enough to make them familiar, and considered altogether, as the source of the moon's light is proved by its waxing and waning.

Letter to Vatier, Feb. 22, 1638. I, 564.

❖ ❖ ❖

I do not know any other way of properly judging the notions which can be taken as principles, except that it is necessary to prepare the mind, getting rid of all the opinions with which one is preoccupied, and rejecting as doubtful all those which can be doubtful.

Letter to Mersenne, Nov. 15, 1638. II, 435.

171

Principles [or first causes] ought to meet two conditions: one, that they be so clear and so evident that the human mind cannot doubt their truth, when it applies itself attentively to the consideration of them; the other, that it is upon them that the knowledge of other things depends, so that they cannot be known without them, but not conversely.

Principles, Preface. IX2, 2.

◈   ◈   ◈

As for common principles, or reasons, for example "it is impossible that the same thing be and not be," men who are governed by their senses, as we all are before philosophy, do not consider them and pay no attention to them; but as these notions are manifestly innate in them, and as they experience them in themselves, they forget them and only consider them confusedly, never in an abstract manner, nor apart from matter and singular objects. If they consider them thus, no one doubts them, and if the sceptics had done so, no one would be a sceptic, because these things cannot be denied by those who consider them with attention.

Burman. V, 146.

PRINCIPLES, FIRST

The first principles themselves are known only by intuition, while ultimate conclusions are known only by deduction.

Rules, III. X, 370.

See *axioms, common notions.*

PROBABLE KNOWLEDGE

We reject all knowledge which is merely probable, and we decide never to believe in anything which is not perfectly known, about which doubt is possible.

Rules, II. X, 362.

172

PROBLEMS, PERFECTLY DETERMINED

Perfectly determined problems contain almost no difficulties, other than those which consist in developing proportions to produce equalities.

Rules, XIV. X, 441.

PROVIDENCE

We ought often to reflect upon the divine Providence, and tell ourselves that it is impossible that anything should ever happen otherwise than it has been determined from all eternity by that Providence; so that it is like a fatality or an immutable necessity, and it is necessary to oppose [the concept of] chance, in order to destroy it, as a chimera which comes only from the error of our understanding.

Passions, II, 145. XI, 438.

PUPIL

The changes in size of the pupil [of the eye] serve to moderate the strength of sight; for it is necessary that it be smaller, when the light is too great, so that fewer rays of light will enter into the eye, and so that the nerve will not be irritated.

Treatise on Man. XI, 157.

◈ ◈ ◈

PURPOSE

It is not at all likely that all things were made for us, in such a way that God had no other goal in creating them. And it would be, it. seems to me, impertinent to want to make use of this opinion as the foundation for the reasoning of physics; for we can hardly doubt that there are an infinity of things now in the world, or rather that there have been before and have already entirely ceased to be, without any man ever seeing or knowing them, and without their ever having served any purpose.

Principles, III, 3. IX2, 104.

◈ ◈ ◈

See causes, final; earth; man; presumption.

QUALITIES

All the qualities which we perceive in the objects of vision can be reduced to six principal ones, which are: light, color, position, distance, size, and shape.

Dioptrics, VI. VI, 130.

◈　◈　◈

See *body; mode.*

QUALITIES, REAL

When [as a child] I conceived weight as a real quality, inherent in and attached to massive and heavy bodies, even though I called it a *quality,* insofar as I connected it to the bodies in which it resided, nevertheless, because I added the word *real,* I actually thought that it was a substance.

Replies, IV. IX, 240.

◈　◈　◈

See *forms, substantial.*

QUALITIES, SENSIBLE

Although I consider nothing in body other than the sizes, the shapes, and the motions of its particles, I nevertheless claim to explain the nature of light, of heat, and of all the other sensible qualities; so that I assume that these qualities are only in our senses, like pleasure and pain, and not in the objects which we sense, in which there are only certain shapes and motions, which cause the sensations that are named light, heat, etc.

Letter to Chanut, Feb. 26, 1649. V, 291-292.

QUANTITY

I distinctly imagine the quantity that the philosophers ordinarily call continuous quantity, or rather extension in length,

Meditations, V. IX, 50.

175

width and depth, which is in that quantity, or rather in the thing to which it is attributed.

QUESTIONS

In all questions it is necessary that there be something which is unknown, without which the inquiry would make no sense.

Rules, XIII. X, 430.

❖   ❖   ❖

By "questions" we understand everything in which truth or falsehood is found.

Rules, XIII. X, 432.

R

RAREFACTION

Whenever we see that a body is rarefied, we ought to think that there are many intervals between its particles, which are filled with some other body.

Principles, II, 6. IX2, 66.

❖　❖　❖

We ought not to have more difficulty in believing that rarefaction takes place as I have said, even though we do not perceive the body which fills [the pores of the rarefied body] by any of our senses, because there is no reason which obliges us to believe that we have to perceive all the bodies which are around us by means of our senses, and because we see that it is very easy to explain it in this way, and because it is impossible to conceive it otherwise.

Principles, II, 7. IX2, 67.

RATS

Rats are engendered or made by accident in garbage.

Letter to Regius, Dec., 1641. III, 460.

REAL DISTINCTION

There can be said to be a real distinction between two substances when each of them can exist without the other.

Replies, II. IX, 125.

REALITY

There are various degrees of reality or entity: for substance has more reality than accident or mode, and infinite substance than finite. This is why there is also more objective reality in the idea of substance than in that of accident, and in the idea of infinite substance than in the idea of finite substance.

Replies, II. IX, 128.

REASON

Anyone who seriously wishes to search out the truth of things

177

should not choose any particular science; for they are all united among themselves by a reciprocal interdependence; rather, he ought to think only of developing the natural light of his reason, not in order to resolve some difficulty or other of the School, but so that his understanding may show to his will the choice that it must make on every occasion of his life.

Rules, I. X, 361.

❖ ❖ ❖

Nothing seems more absurd to me than to dispute rashly about the secrets of nature, about the influence of the stars upon our inferior regions, about the prediction of the future, and other things of that kind, as so many people do, without ever having asked whether human reason is capable of resolving these questions.

Rules, VIII. X, 398.

❖ ❖ ❖

The power of right judgment, and of distinguishing the true from the false, which is properly what is called good sense or reason, is naturally equal in every man.

Discourse, I. VI, 2.

❖ ❖ ❖

I would believe that reason, insofar as it is the only thing which makes us men, and distinguishes us from the beasts, is entirely complete in everyone.

Discourse, I. VI, 2.

❖ ❖ ❖

Reason is a universal instrument, which can be used in all kinds of situations.

Discourse, V. VI, 57.

❖ ❖ ❖

Not only do beasts have less reason than men; they do not have it at all.

Discourse, V. VI, 58.

❖ ❖ ❖

If we always do everything that our reason dictates to us, we will never have any cause for repenting, even though the

178

outcome makes us see, afterward, that we were deceived, because [the error] is not our fault.

Letter to Elisabeth, Aug. 4, 1645. IV, 266.

❖   ❖   ❖

It is not necessary that our reason never deceive us; it is enough that our conscience testify that we have never lacked resolution and virtue, to execute all the things that we have judged best, and thus virtue alone is sufficient to make us content in this life.

Letter to Elisabeth, Aug 4, 1645. IV, 266-267.

❖   ❖   ❖

The true use of our reason for the conduct of our life consists only in examining and considering without passion the value of all the perfections, those of body as well as those of the mind, which can be acquired by our conduct, such that, since we are ordinarily obliged to deprive ourselves of some of them, in order to have the others, we always choose the best.

Letter to Elisabeth, Sept. 1, 1645. IV, 286-287.

❖   ❖   ❖

As we were born men before we became Christians, it is beyond belief that any man should seriously embrace opinions which he thinks contrary to the right reason that constitutes a man, in order that he may cling to the faith through which he is a Christian.

Notes against a Program, IV. VIII 2, 353-354.

❖   ❖   ❖

What knowledge we have or acquire by the route that our reason takes has, first, the murkiness of the principles from which it is derived, and, in addition, the uncertainty which we find in all our reasonings.

Letter to Newcastle, Mar. or Apr., 1648. V, 137.

See *intuition; natural light.*

REASON, BEINGS OF

It is not true [that God is a being of reason] if by *being of reason* one understands something which does not exist, but only

179

if all the operations of the understanding are taken as *beings of reason,* that is, as beings which share in reason.

Replies, II. IX, 106.

REASON, DISTINCTIONS OF

The distinctions of reason [or distinctions made by thought] consist in the fact that we sometimes distinguish a substance from some one of its attributes, even though it is not possible for us to have a distinct knowledge of it; or rather in the fact that we try to separate two such attributes from the same substance while thinking of one without thinking of the other.

Principles, I, 62. IX2, 53.

REASON, FORMAL

I proved nothing else by the example of the wax [in the second Meditation] than that the color, the hardness, the shape, etc., did not belong to the formal reason of the wax, i.e., that one could conceive everything that could be found to be necessarily in the wax, without having need of thinking of these.

Replies, III. IX, 136.

REASON, NATURAL

Those who use only their pure natural reason will better judge my opinions than those who believe only in ancient books.

Discourse, VI. VI, 77.

REASONING

Because there are some men who despise reasoning, even in connection with the simplest matters in geometry, and make errors there, judging that I was subject to failure as much as anyone else, I rejected as false all the reasonings that I had previously taken for demonstrations.

Discourse, IV. VI, 32.

REFRACTION

In order to determine their quantity [i.e. measure refraction], insofar as it depends upon the particular nature of the bodies in which it takes place, it is necessary to go to experience.

Dioptrics, II. VI, 102.

REFUTE

There are only two ways to refute what I have written: one

is to prove by some experiments or reasons that the things which I have supposed are false; and the other that what I have deduced from these suppositions should not have been deduced.

Letter to Mersenne, May 17, 1638. II, 143.

REGRET

Regret is a species of sadness, which has a particular bitterness, in that it is always joined to some despair, and to the memory of the pleasure that enjoyment has given us.

Passions, III, 209. XI, 484-485.

RELATIVE

As for the *relative,* it is that which participates in the same nature, or at least in some one of its aspects; because of this it may be connected to the absolute, and be deduced from it through a chain of reasonings; but, in addition, it contains in its concept other things which I call *relations*: of this nature is everything which is called dependent, effect, composite, particular, multiple, unequal, dissimilar, oblique, etc.

Rules, VI. X, 382.

See *absolute.*

REMORSE

If one determines to do some action before irresolution has been overcome, that gives birth to remorse of conscience: it does not have to do with the time to come, as do the preceding passions, but with the present or the past.

Passions, II, 60. XI, 376.

❖   ❖   ❖

Remorse of conscience is a species of sadness, which comes from the suspicion that something that one is doing, or has done, is not good.

Passions, III, 177. XI, 464.

REPENTANCE

It seems to me that there is no reason for repentance if one has done what he judged to be the best at the time when he had to resolve upon its execution, even though, afterward, rethinking it with greater leisure, he judges it to have been an error. But one ought rather to repent if he has done something

181

against his own conscience, even though he recognizes later that he has done better than he thought he had.

Letter to Elisabeth, Oct. 6, 1645. IV, 307.

❖ ❖ ❖

[Repentance] is a Christian virtue, which serves for the correction, not only of faults which are committed voluntarily, but also those which have been commited through ignorance, when some passion has prevented one from knowing the truth.

Letter to Elisabeth, Nov. 3, 1645. IV, 331.

❖ ❖ ❖

Repentance is directly contrary to self-satisfaction; and it is a species of sadness which comes from the fact that one believes himself to have done some evil act; and it is very bitter, because its cause comes only from ourselves.

Passions, III, 191. XI, 472.

❖ ❖ ❖

See *satisfaction*.

REPUTATION

I fear reputation more than I desire it, judging that it always manages to diminish the freedom and leisure of those who acquire it, and I have such perfect freedom and leisure, and value them so much, that there is no Monarch in the world who is rich enough to buy them from me.

Letter to Mersenne, Apr. 15, 1630. I, 136.

REST

The philosophers attribute to the smallest motion a condition which is much more solid and true than they do to rest, which they say is only a privation. As for me, I conceive that rest is a quality, which ought to be attributed to matter as long as it remains in one place, just as motion is a quality which is attributed to it when it changes place.

The World, VII. XI, 40.

I consider matter, left to itself and not receiving any impulse from elsewhere, as perfectly at rest.

Letter to More, Aug., 1649. V, 404.

REVELATION, DIVINE

Divine revelation gives us a certainty which is superior to every other kind of knowledge, since the faith that we give to it, even when it is obscure, is not an act of the intellect, but of the will.

Rules, III. X, 370.

RICH

A man who has only a thousand pistoles would be quite rich, if there were no other persons in the world who had more; and the same man would be quite poor, if there were no one in the world who did not have much more.

Letter to Chanut, June 6, 1647. V, 55.

RIDICULE

As for modest ridicule, which usefully reproves vice by making it appear ridiculous, yet without laughing at it, nor bearing witness to any hate against persons: this is not a passion, but a quality of a good man, which brings out his sense of humor, and the tranquility of his soul, which are marks of virtue; and often also the cleverness of his mind, insofar as he gives an amusing appearance to the things which he ridicules.

Passions, III, 180. XI, 465-466.

◈   ◈   ◈

RING

In every motion there must be a circle or ring of bodies which move together.

Principles, II, 33. IX2, 81.

◈   ◈   ◈

See *vortex*.

ROCKS

I do not know anything in particular concerning the generation of rocks, except that I distinguish them from metals, in that the tiny particles which make up the metals are notably larger than theirs.

Letter to Newcastle, Nov. 23, 1646. IV, 570.

RULES

The maxims of the sages can be reduced to a very small number of general rules.

Cogitationes Privatae. X, 217.

❖   ❖   ❖

A large number of rules often shows the inexperience of the teacher, and if one can reduce them to a single, general precept, it is more concise than stating them as a large number of separate rules.

Rules, XVIII. X, 461.

RUMOR

[To Rumor:] You are so accustomed to lying when you precede us, that the wisest persons usually judge the truth to be the contrary of what you would have people believe.

Birth of Peace, XIV.

S

SAD HUMOR

The *sad humor* is composed of slowness and disquiet, and can be augmented by malignity and timidity.

Treatise on Man. XI, 167.

SADNESS

Sadness is a disagreeable languor, which consists in the annoyance that the soul receives from evil, or from some fault, which the impressions of the brain represent to it as pertaining to it. And there is also an intellectual sadness, which is not a passion, but which is almost always accompanied by it.

Passions, II, 92. XI, 397.

❖ ❖ ❖

In sadness, the pulse is feeble and weak, and something like cords are felt about the heart, which press against it, and ice which freezes it, and communicates its coldness to the rest of the body; and nevertheless one often retains a good appetite, and senses that the stomach still does its job, provided that there is no hate mixed with the sadness.

Passions, II, 100. XI, 403.

❖ ❖ ❖

Often, after having laughed a great deal, one naturally feels inclined to sadness, because the more fluid part of the blood from the spleen has been exhausted, and the other, thicker blood follows it to the heart.

Passions, II, 126. XI, 421.

❖ ❖ ❖

See *joy*.

SALT

Sometimes it happens that the salt which comes from the sea passes through the pores of the earth which are so narrow, or so arranged that they change something in the shape of the particles of salt, by means of which it loses the form of common salt, and takes on that of saltpeter, sal ammoniac, or some other kind of salt.

Principles, IV, 69. IX2, 238.

SATISFACTION

We can also consider the cause of good or evil when it is as much present as past. And the good which has been done by ourselves gives us an internal satisfaction, which is the sweetest of all the passions; on the other hand, evil excites repentance, which is the bitterest.

Passions, II, 63.

❖   ❖   ❖

The satisfaction, which those who constantly follow the path of virtue always have, is a habit in their soul, which is called tranquility and ease of conscience. But that which is newly acquired, when one has just done some action which he thinks is good, is a passion, namely a species of joy, which I believe to be the sweetest of all, because its cause depends only upon ourselves.

Passions, III, 190. XI, 471.

SCEPTICS

I did not imitate the sceptics, who doubt only for the sake of doubting, and always pretend to be irresolute.

Discourse, III. VI, 29.

SCHOLASTICISM

In case anyone is put out by this new use of the term intuition and of other terms which in the following pages I am similarly compelled to dissever from their current meaning, I here make the general announcement that I pay no attention to the way in which particular terms have of late been employed in the schools, because it would have been difficult to employ the same terminology while my theory was wholly different.

Rules, III. X, 369.

The monks have given birth to all the sects and to all the heresies, by their theology, that is, by their scholasticism, which must be destroyed before anything else.

Burman. V, 176.

SCHOOLS

We very often see that people who have never troubled themselves with study make clearer and more solid judgments than those who have passed their time in the schools.

Rules, IV. X, 371.

SCIENCE

I do not want to give the public another Lullian *Ars Brevis,* but a science with new foundations, which permits a general resolution of all questions which can be proposed, for any type of quantity, continuous or discontinuous, but each according to its own nature.

To Beeckman, Mar. 26, 1619. X, 156-57.

◈   ◈   ◈

Science is like a wife; if, modestly, she remains close to her husband, she is honored; if she gives herself to everyone, she cheapens herself.

Cogitationes Privatae. X, 214.

◈   ◈   ◈

The sciences are now masked; if the masks were removed, they would appear in all their beauty.

Cogitationes Privatae. X, 215.

◈   ◈   ◈

Determinate limits are prescribed for all minds: they cannot go beyond them. If certain persons, by default of mind, cannot use principles of invention, they will be able at least to know the true price of the sciences; and that will be enough to provide them with true judgments about the value of things.

Cogitationes Privatae. X, 215.

◈   ◈   ◈

Since the sciences taken all together are identical with human wisdom, which always remains one and the same, however

187

applied to different subjects, and suffers no more differentiation proceeding from them than the light of the sun experiences from the variety of the things which it illuminates, there is no need for minds to be confined at all within limits.

Rules, I. X, 360.

◈　◈　◈

All science is certain and evident knowledge.

Rules, II. X, 362.

◈　◈　◈

One ought to derive the sciences — even the most profoundly hidden ones — not from imposing and obscure principles, but only from principles which are easy and quite close at hand.

Rules, IX. X, 402.

◈　◈　◈

All human science consists of one thing: namely, the distinct vision of the way in which simple natures combine together in the composition of other things.

Rules, XII. X, 427.

◈　◈　◈

The knowledge of the order [of the positions of the stars] is the key and the foundation of the highest and most perfect Science that men can have concerning material things; so much so that by means of this science one could know *a priori* all the various forms and essences of terrestrial bodies, rather than, without it, being forced to content ourselves with guessing at them *a posteriori*, and by their effects.

Letter to Mersenne, May 10, 1632. I, 250-251.

◈　◈　◈

By [mathematical] science I understand the ability to resolve all questions, and to discover by one's own labor everything that the human mind can find in that science.

Letter to Hogelande, Feb. 8, 1640.

◈　◈　◈

Our nature is such that we are deceived in things which are the most evident, and as consequence we would not have a true *science* but a simple *persuasion* even at the moment when we had derived [conclusions] from these [first] principles.

Letter to Regius, May 24, 1640. III, 64-65.

188

Thus [without the knowledge of God] I would never have a true and certain science of anything whatever, but only vague and inconstant opinions.

Meditations, V. IX, 55.

❖   ❖   ❖

The certainty and the truth of every science depend only on the knowledge of the true God: so that before I knew this, I could not know any other thing perfectly.

Meditations, V. IX, 56.

❖   ❖   ❖

I do not deny that an atheist could know clearly that the three angles of a triangle are equal to two right angles; but I maintain only that he does not know it by a true and certain science, because any piece of knowledge which can be rendered doubtful ought not to be called science.

Replies, II. IX, 111.

❖   ❖   ❖

As for the sciences, which are nothing but the certain judgments that we base upon some preceding knowledge, some are derived from common things, which everyone has heard about, and others from rare and erudite experiments.

Search for Truth. X, 503.

❖   ❖   ❖

See *mathematics, universal; persuasion.*

SCORN

See *esteem.*

SCRIPTURE

I believe that it is to apply Holy Scripture to an end for which God has not given it, and as a consequence to abuse it, to want to derive from it the knowledge of truths which belong only to human sciences, and which do not serve for our salvation.

Letter to ❋❋❋, *Aug., 1638 (?). II, 348.*

SECRET

As soon as I see the word *secret* [*arcanum*] in some proposition, I begin to have a bad opinion of it.

Letter to Mersenne, Nov. 20, 1629. I, 78.

SECURITY

When hope is so strong that it entirely eliminates fear, it changes its nature and is called security or assurance. And when one is assured that what one wishes will come to pass, even though he continues to wish that it happen, he ceases nevertheless to be agitated by the passions of desire, which looks at the outcome with disquiet.

Passions, III, 166. XI, 457.

SEEDS OF KNOWLEDGE

See *poets*.

SEEDS OF THOUGHT

The human mind actually possesses something divine, in which the first seeds of thought have been implanted, so that they often produce their fruit spontaneously, however much they may have been neglected and stifled by study.

Rules, IV. X, 373.

SEEDS OF TRUTH

I am persuaded that certain primary seeds of truth are implanted by nature in the human mind, and that we suffocate them in us by reading and hearing so many errors of every sort; but these seeds grew so well in that rude and simple world of the ancients that the same mental light which showed them that they must prefer virtue to pleasure, and honesty to expediency, even though they did not know why this was so, also gave them true ideas in philosophy and mathematics, although they never were able to perfect these sciences.

Rules, IV. X, 376.

❖   ❖   ❖

See *first notions*.

SELF-CAUSED

The words *self-caused* cannot in any way whatever be understood of the efficient cause, but solely [in such a way] that the inexhaustible power of God is the cause or the reason by which he has no need of cause.

Replies, IV. IX, 182.

See *being by itself*.

SENSATION

It is the soul which senses, and not the body: for it is easy to see that, when it is diverted by an ecstatic or deep contemplation, the whole body remains without sensation, even though various objects touch it.

Dioptrics, IV. VI, 109.

❖   ❖   ❖

I do not recognize any other sensation than that which takes place in the brain.

Letter to Plempius, Oct. 3, 1637. I, 420.

❖   ❖   ❖

There is found in me a certain passive faculty of sensation, i.e., of receiving and knowing the ideas of sensible things; but it would be useless to me, and I could not make use of it in any way, if there were not in me, or in another, an active faculty, capable of forming and producing these ideas.

Meditations, VI. IX, 63.

❖   ❖   ❖

Actually, all the sensations of hunger, thirst, pain, etc., are nothing other than certain confused ways of thinking, which come from and depend upon the union and, as it were, the mixture, of the mind with the body.

Meditations, VI. IX, 64.

❖   ❖   ❖

We perceive that the sensations of pain, and all others of similar nature, are not pure thoughts of the soul as distinct from the body, but confused perceptions of that soul which is really united to the body.

Letter to Regius, Jan., 1642(?). III, 493.

◈ ◈ ◈

We can have a clear and distinct knowledge of the sensations, the emotions [*affections*] and the appetites, provided that we are careful not to include in the judgments that we base upon them more than what we know precisely by means of our understanding and of which we are assured by reason.

Principles, I, 66. IX2, 55.

◈ ◈ ◈

In order that we may distinguish here what is clear in our sensations from what is obscure, we note, in the first place, that we clearly and distinctly know pain, color, and the other sensations, when we consider them simply as thoughts; but that, when we wish to judge that color, pain, etc., are things which subsist outside our thought, we do not conceive in any way what thing it is that is color, pain, etc.

Principles, I, 68. IX2, 56.

◈ ◈ ◈

It is the various thoughts of our soul, which immediately follow the motions which are excited by the ends of the nerves in the brain, which we properly call our sensations, or rather the perceptions of our senses.

Principles, IV, 189. IX2, 310.

◈ ◈ ◈

I distinguish seven principal sensations, two of which can be called internal [natural appetites and passions], and the five others external [touch, taste, odor, hearing and sight].

Principles, IV, 190. IX2, 311.

◈ ◈ ◈

There is nothing in bodies which can excite any sensation in us, other than motion, shape or place, and the size of their particles.

Principles, IV, 198. IX2, 316.

◈ ◈ ◈

The human soul separated from the body does not properly have sensation.

Letter to More, Aug., 1649. V, 402.

[The passions] can be called sensations, because they are received in the soul in the same way as are the objects of the external senses, and are not otherwise known by the soul.

Passions, I, 28. XI, 350.

❖   ❖   ❖

See *body; passions.*

SENSES

Although our external senses are applied to their objects through an action [or, more precisely, through a local motion], insofar as they are parts of the body, they never sense, properly speaking, other than passively, just as the wax receives the image from the seal.

Rules, XII. X, 412.

❖   ❖   ❖

All the conduct of our life depends upon our senses, among which that of sight is the most universal and the most noble.

Discourse, VI. VI, 81.

❖   ❖   ❖

The ideas that I received by the senses were much more lively, more precise, and even in their own way more distinct, than any of those which I could suppose by myself in meditation, or which I found imprinted in my memory.

Meditations, VI. IX, 60.

❖   ❖   ❖

Everything that we perceive by means of our senses is related to the strict union of the soul with the body, and we ordinarily know by means of the senses what can be profitable or harmful to us in the external body, but not the nature of the body, except perhaps rarely and accidentally.

Principles, II, 3. IX 2, 64-65.

❖   ❖   ❖

As for the external senses, everyone customarily counts five, because there are five different types of object which move the nerves, and because the impressions which come from these objects excite five different kinds of confused thoughts in the soul.

Principles, IV, 191. IX2, 312.

❖ ❖ ❖

The soul does not sense insofar as it is in each part of the body, but solely insofar as it is in the brain, where the nerves, by their movements, communicate to it the various actions of the external objects which touch the parts of the body in which these nerves are inserted.

Principles, IV, 196. IX2, 314.

❖ ❖ ❖

See *consider.*

SENSE, COMMON

The common sense [is] where the ideas are received.

Discourse, V. VI, 55.

❖ ❖ ❖

It is certain that the seat of the common sense ought to be quite mobile, in order to receive all the impressions which come from the senses; but it ought to be such that it can be moved only by the [animal] spirits, which transmit these impressions, and the *conarium* [pineal gland] alone is of this sort.

Letter to Mersenne, Apr. 21. 1641. III, 362.

❖ ❖ ❖

That faculty which is usually termed the *common sense* [is that] whereby impressions are received of imaginary things as much as of real things, so that they affect the mind—a faculty which philosophers commonly allow even to the brute creation.

Notes against a Program, VII. VIII 2, 356.

SENSE, GOOD

Good sense is the best-divided thing in the world: because everyone thinks that he is so well provided with it that even those who are most difficult to please in everything else do not usually want more of it than they have.

Discourse, I. VI, 1-2.

$\diamond \quad \diamond \quad \diamond$

Just as there is nothing good in this world, except for good sense, which can be called absolutely good, there is also no evil, from which one cannot derive some advantage, if one has good sense.

Letter to Elisabeth, June, 1645. IV, 237.

$\diamond \quad \diamond \quad \diamond$

See *reason*.

SERVILITY

As for servility, or vicious humility, it consists principally in that one thinks himself feeble and irresolute and that, as if he did not have the full use of his free will, he cannot prevent himself from doing things about which he knows that he will repent afterward; and also, in that he believes that he cannot subsist by himself, nor get along without many things, whose acquisition depends upon another.

Passions, III, 159. XI, 450.

SEX

With the difference in sex, which nature has given to men, as to the animals without reason, she has also given certain impressions in the brain, which, at a certain age and in certain times, make one consider himself as defective, and as if he were only the half of a whole, of which a person of the other sex ought to be the other half; in such a way that the acquisition of that half is confusedly represented by nature as the greatest of all the goods which can be imagined.

Passions, II, 90. XI, 395-396.

SHAME

Shame is composed of self-love and a pressing desire to avoid present infamy.

Passions, II, 117. XI, 415.

$\diamond \quad \diamond \quad \diamond$

Shame is a species of sadness, founded upon the love of oneself, which comes from the opinion or fear that one will be blamed.

Passions, III, 205. XI, 482.

See *pride*.

SHAPE

Nothing is more easily sensed than shape: one actually touches it and sees it.

Rules, XII. X, 413.

◈ ◈ ◈

The infinite number of shapes is sufficient to express all the differences among sensible things.

Rules, XII. X, 413.

◈ ◈ ◈

We judge the shape of an object by our knowledge, or opinion, of the position of the various parts of the object, and not by their resemblance to pictures which are in the eye: for these pictures ordinarily only contain ovals and diamond-shapes, when they make us see circles and squares.

Dioptrics, VI. VI, 140.

◈ ◈ ◈

The idea of shape is joined to the idea of extension and of substance, since it is impossible for me to conceive a shape, while denying that it has an extension, nor to conceive an extension, while denying that it is the extension of a substance.

Letter to Gibieuf, Jan. 19, 1642. III, 475.

◈ ◈ ◈

It is not possible to conceive of shapes which do not have extension.

Rules, XII. X, 421.

SHREWDNESS

For me, the maxim that I have most often observed in all the conduct of my life, has been always to live virtuously and to believe that the principal shrewdness [*finesse*] is never to want to use shrewdness.

Letter to Elisabeth, Jan., 1646. IV, 357.

SIGHT

The sense [of sight] also depends in this machine [the body] upon two nerves, which must doubtless be composed of many tiny threads, the finest, and the easiest to move, that any can be; since they have as their end to report to the brain the various actions of the particles of the second element [air], which, following what I have said above, will give occasion to the soul, when it is united to the machine, to conceive the various ideas of colors and of light.

Treatise on Man. XII, 151.

❖   ❖   ❖

The most subtle of all the senses is that of sight; for the optic nerves, which are its organs, are not moved by the air, nor by the other terrestrial bodies, but solely by the particles of the second element, which, passing through the pores of all the fluids and transparent membranes of the eyes, travel to these nerves, and, depending on the various ways in which they move it, make the soul sense all the variety of colors and of light.

Principles, IV, 195. IX2, 314.

SIGNS

Whatever does not require the immediate attention of the mind, which is nevertheless necessary for the conclusion of an argument, it is better to designate by very brief signs, rather than by complete figures.

Rules, XVI. X, 454.

❖   ❖   ❖

Each thing that we must consider as a unit in order to resolve a difficulty can be designated by a unique sign, which can be made in any form we wish.

Rules, XVI. X, 455.

SIMPLE

Conscious as I am of my inadequacy, I have resolved that in my investigation into truth I shall follow obstinately such an order as will require me first to start with what is simplest and easiest, and never permit me to proceed farther until in the first sphere there seems to be nothing more to be done.

Rules, IV. X, 378-379.

❖   ❖   ❖

We ought to give the whole of our attention to the simplest and most easily mastered things, and remain a long time in contemplation of them until we are accustomed to intuit the truth clearly and distinctly.

Rules, IX. X, 400.

❖   ❖   ❖

Concerning things only insofar as they are conceived by the understanding, we call only those things "simple" which are known so clearly and distinctly that the mind cannot divide them into others which would be more distinctly known: of this nature are shape, extension, movement, etc.

Rules, XII. X, 418.

❖   ❖   ❖

One cannot give any logical definition [of truth] which helps to know its nature. And I believe the same of many other things, which are quite simple and naturally known, such as shape, size, movement, place, time, etc., such that when one wishes to define these things, he obscures them and gets entangled.

Letter to Mersenne, Oct. 16, 1639. II, 597.

❖   ❖   ❖

There are many things [e.g., doubt, thought, existence] which we make more obscure when we wish to define them, because, as they are very simple and very clear, it is impossible for us to know them and comprehend them better than by themselves.

Search for Truth. X, 523-524.

❖   ❖   ❖

It is impossible to apprehend these [simple] things otherwise than by oneself, and to be persuaded otherwise than by his own experience, and by that conscience or interior witness which each man finds in himself when he examines any observation whatever; in such a way that, as it would be useless to define the color white to make a blind man understand, while for us to know it, it is enough to open our eyes and to see white, in the same way, to know what doubt and thought are, it is enough to doubt and to think.

Search for Truth. X, 524.

A composite entity is one in which are found two or more attributes, any one of which can be comprehended distinctly apart from the other, for it is from the fact that one can be thus known without the other that each of these constituent elements is seen to be, not a mode of the others, but a thing, or the attribute of a thing which can exist without that attribute. A simple entity is one in which such attributes are not found.

Notes against a Program, II. VIII 2, 350.

SIMPLE IDEAS

I do not completely understand the question that you ask me, namely whether our ideas are expressed by a simple term; for since words are the invention of men, one can always use one or many to explain the same thing; but I have explained in my Reply to the First Objections how a triangle inscribed in a square can be taken for a single idea or for many.

Letter to Mersenne, July 23, 1641. III, 417-418.

SIMPLE NATURES

Everything that we can know is composed of simple natures.

Rules, XII. X, 420.

◈ ◈ ◈

The simple natures are completely known in themselves, and they never contain anything false.

Rules, XII. X, 420.

◈ ◈ ◈

We can never understand anything other than the simple natures, and the sort of mixture or composition which can be made from them.

Rules, XII. X, 422.

◈ ◈ ◈

No effort is required to know the simple natures, because they are sufficiently known in themselves.

Rules, XII. X, 425.

SIMPLE NOTIONS

We cannot seek the simple notions anywhere other than in

our soul, which has them all in itself by its nature, but which does not always sufficiently distinguish one from another, or does not attribute them to the objects to which it should attribute them.

Letter to Elisabeth, May 21, 1643. III, 666-667.

❖ ❖ ❖

When I said that the proposition, *I think, therefore I am,* is the first and most certain which presents itself to anyone who thinks in an orderly fashion, I did not for that reason deny that it was necessary to know in advance what thought, certainty, and existence were, and that in order to think one must exist, and other similar things; but, because these notions are so simple that, by themselves, they do not give us any knowledge of anything that exists, I did not judge that they had to be taken into consideration.

Principles, I, 10. IX2, 29.

❖ ❖ ❖

See *primitive notions.*

SIMPLE THINGS

Of this type of thing [i.e., simple things] is corporeal nature in general, and its extension; together with the shape of extended things, their quantity or size, and their number; as also the place where they are, the time which measures their duration, and other similar things.

Meditations, I. IX, 15.

SIN

In everything where there is occasion to sin, there is indifference; and I do not believe that, to do wrong, there is need to see clearly that what we do is evil; it is enough to see it confusedly, or solely to recall that we have judged previously that it was, without seeing it in any way, that is, without paying attention to the reasons which prove it; for, if we saw it clearly, it would be impossible to sin, during the time that we saw it in that way; that is why it is said that every sinner is one through ignorance.

Letter to Mesland, May 2, 1644(?). IV, 117.

◈　　◈　　◈

Sin actually results, in general, from ignorance, because no one can desire evil, insofar as it is evil.

Burman. V, 159.

SIZE

Size does not differ from that which has a given size, and number does not differ from what is numbered, except in our thought.

Principles, II, 8. IX2, 67.

SKY

Let us suppose that the matter of the sky is liquid, as well as that which composes the sun and the fixed stars.

Principles, III, 24. IX2, 112.

SLEEP

During sleep, the substance of the brain, which is resting, has the leisure to be nourished and repaired, since it is moistened by the blood which is contained in the tiny veins or arteries which appear in its exterior surface.

Treatise on Man. XI, 198.

◈　　◈　　◈

I believe [the cause of sleep] to consist in the fact that, just as we see, sometimes, that the sails of ships fold up, because the wind does not have enough force to fill them, in the same way the animal spirits, which come from the heart, are no longer abundant enough to fill the marrow of the brain, and hold open all the pores; which then makes us sleep.

Letter to Newcastle, Apr., 1645(?). IV, 192.

SLEEPING

There are no conclusive indices, nor very certain marks, by which one can distinguish waking from sleeping.

Meditations, I. IX, 15.

SMOKE

Small particles of wood, mixed with air, compose the smoke, as the larger particles of the wood compose the ashes.

Letter to Mersenne, Oct. 20, 1642. III, 587.

SNOW

I will not forget [the snow] whose particles have the shape of tiny six-pointed stars very perfectly proportioned, and which, even though they were not observed by the ancients, are nevertheless one of the rarest marvels of nature.

Meteorology, I. VI, 232.

SOCRATES

When we consider the ignorance, or rather the doubt of Socrates, we find that it became a question [for inquiry] as soon as Socrates, turning toward that doubt, began to ask whether it is true that he doubted all things, and replied affirmatively.

Rules, XIII. X, 432.

SOLES

Since the soles of our feet are accustomed to a rather heavy touch, because of the weight of the body that they sustain, we hardly sense that touch when we are walking; on the other hand, a very light and soft touch, when they are tickled, is almost unbearable to us, simply because it is not the ordinary thing for us.

Passions, II, 72. XI, 382.

SOLID

I do not find any difference between solid bodies and liquid bodies other than the fact that the particles of the one can be separated from the whole much more easily than those of the other.

The World, III. XI, 13

SOLIDITY

On this earth, pieces of gold, of lead, or of some other metal, conserve their agitation [i.e., state of motion] well, and have much more force with which to continue their motion, when they are once moved, than have pieces of wood or stones of the same size and shape, which makes us judge that they are more solid: that is, that these metals have more of the matter of the third element in them, and fewer pores which are filled with the matter of the first or second element.

Principles, III, 122. IX2, 175.

SOPHISMS

The subtlest sophisms ordinarily deceive almost no one who makes use of pure and simple reason, but deceive only the sophists themselves.

Rules, X. X, 406.

SOUL

When the *rational soul* is in this machine [the body], it will have its principal seat in the brain.

Treatise on Man. XI, 131.

❖ ❖ ❖

The soul is a substance distinct from the body, whose nature is nothing other than thinking.

Letter to Mersenne, Feb. 27, 1637. I, 349.

❖ ❖ ❖

The soul is a being or substance which is not at all bodily, and its nature is only thinking; it is the first thing that one can know with certainty.

Letter to °°°, May, 1637. I, 353.

❖ ❖ ❖

This ego, that is, the soul by which I am what I am, is entirely distinct from the body, and it is even easier to know than the body, and even if the body did not exist, the soul would not cease to be what it is.

Discourse, IV. VI, 33.

❖ ❖ ❖

The rational soul cannot in any way be derived from the potentiality of matter, as can the other things about which I have spoken, but it must have been expressly created; and it is not enough that it be located in the human body like a pilot in his ship, except perhaps to move its limbs, but it must also be joined and united more closely with the body in order to have,

203

beyond that, sensations and appetites similar to ours, and thus to compose a true man.

Discourse, V. VI, 59.

❖ ❖ ❖

Our [soul] is of a nature which is entirely independent of the body and, as a consequence, it is not subject to dying with it.

Discourse, V. VI, 59.

❖ ❖ ❖

The soul, residing in the brain, can thus, by the intermediary of the nerves, receive impressions from external objects.

Dioptrics, IV. VI, 109.

❖ ❖ ❖

From the fact alone that one conceives clearly and distinctly the two natures of the soul and the body as diverse, one knows that truly they *are diverse,* and, as a consequence, that the soul can think without the body, even though, when it is joined to the body, it can be disturbed in its operations by the malfunctioning of the body's organs.

Letter to Reneri, Apr.-May, 1638. II, 38.

❖ ❖ ❖

I prefer to think that the wax, simply because of its flexibility, receives all sorts of shapes, and that the soul acquires all its knowledge by the reflection that it makes, either upon itself concerning intellectual things, or upon the various dispositions of the brain to which it is joined, concerning corporeal things, whether these dispositions depend upon the senses or upon other causes.

Letter to Mersenne, Oct. 16, 1639. II, 598.

❖ ❖ ❖

Anima [soul] in good Latin signifies air, or the wind from the mouth; from which I believe that it has been transferred to signify the mind, and it is for that reason that I said that it is often taken to be a corporeal thing.

Letter to Mersenne, Apr. 21, 1641. III, 362.

❖ ❖ ❖

I do not admit that the *vegetative and sensitive force* in the brutes merits the name of soul, as the *soul* merits that name in man; but the common people have wished it thus, because they have not known that the beasts have no *soul* and as a consequence the name *soul* is equivocal with regard to man and beast.

Letter to Regius, May, 1641. III, 370.

❖   ❖   ❖

There is only one *soul* in man, i.e., the *rational soul*; because the only human actions that should be counted are those which depend on reason. With regard to the *vegetative and motive force of the body* to which they [the Aristotelians] give the name of vegetative and sensitive soul in the plants and in the brutes, they are also in man; but they should not be called *souls* in man, because they are not the first principle of his actions, and they are of quite a different type from the rational soul.

Letter to Regius, May, 1641. III, 371.

❖   ❖   ❖

I have demonstrated that the soul is nothing other than a thing which thinks; it is therefore impossible that we can ever think of anything without having at the same time the idea of our soul, as of a thing capable of thinking of all that we think about.

Letter to Mersenne, July, 1641. III, 394.

❖   ❖   ❖

The human body can easily perish, but the mind, or the soul of man (I do not distinguish between them), is immortal by its very nature.

Meditations, Summary. IX, 10.

❖   ❖   ❖

It is certain that this ego, that is, my soul, by which I am what I am, is entirely and truly distinct from my body, and that it could be or exist without it.

Meditations, VI. IX, 62.

❖   ❖   ❖

The reason for my belief that the soul always thinks is the same that makes me believe that light always lights, even

205

though there are no eyes that see it; that warmth is always warm, even though no one is warmed by it; that body, or extended substance, always has extension; and generally, that whatever constitutes the nature of a thing is always in it, as long as it exists; so that it would be easier for me to believe that the soul stopped existing, when one says that it stops thinking, than to believe that it exists without thinking.

Letter to Gibieuf, Jan. 19, 1642. III, 478.

❖   ❖   ❖

The numerical unity of the body of a man does not depend upon its matter, but upon its form, which is the soul.

Letter to Mesland, 1645 or 1646. IV, 346.

❖   ❖   ❖

If [beasts] thought as we do, they would have an immortal soul as we do; but this is not plausible, because there is no reason for believing this of some animals without believing it of all, and because there are many animals which are too imperfect for us to believe it of them, like the oysters, the sponges, etc.

Letter to Newcastle, Nov. 23, 1646. IV, 576.

❖   ❖   ❖

[The properties of the soul] are all to be subordinated to two predominant properties, one of which is the perception of the understanding, the other the determination of the will.

Notes against a Program, XVI. VIII 2, 363.

❖   ❖   ❖

The soul, being a thinking thing, is also, besides thought, a substance which thinks.

Burman. V, 156.

SOUL AND BODY

At the first moment that our soul was joined to the body, it is likely that it sensed joy, and immediately afterward, love; then perhaps also hate, and sadness.

Letter to Chanut, Feb. 1, 1647. IV, 604.

❖   ❖   ❖

There is a connection between our soul and our body such that when we have once joined some corporeal action with some thought, one of the two is never afterward presented to us, without the other being presented also.

Passions, II, 107. XI, 407.

See *sensations, passions.*

SOUL, RATIONAL AND SENSITIVE

It is only the clash between the movements that the body tends to excite, by means of its [animal] spirits, and those the soul makes by means of its will, at the same time in the [pineal] gland, which is customarily imagined to constitute all the combats between the inferior part of the soul, which is called sensitive, and the superior part, which is rational, or between the natural appetites and the will. For there is only one soul in us, and that soul does not have various parts: the same soul that is sensitive is rational, and all its appetites are acts of will.

Passions, I, 47. XI, 364.

SOUND

The most notable properties of sound are two, namely, its differences with respet to time or duration, and with respect to the force or intensity of sound, considered insofar as it is low or high.

Compendium Musicae. X, 89.

❖   ❖   ❖

One sound is to another as one string [on a musical intrument] is to another; for each string contains in itself all the other lengths of string which are less than itself, and none of those which are greater. As a consequence, then, all the higher sounds are contained in the lower, but the reverse is not true: all the lower sounds are not contained in the higher.

Compendium Musicae. X, 97.

❖   ❖   ❖

And note that a single [vibration] cannot make any one hear anything other than a dull sound, which passes away in a moment, and in which there is no variation, other than being louder or softer, according to whether the ear is struck harder or more softly; but that, when many such blows follow one another, one can see with the naked eye that the strings of an instrument vibrate, and that bells shake when they resound; and these tiny shakings compose a sound, which the soul judges sweeter or cruder, according to whether they are more or less equal among themselves.

Treatise on Man. XI, 149-150.

❖ ❖ ❖

I judge that the experiment is correct, which shows that sounds do not travel more quickly with the wind than against the wind; for the movement of sound is something quite different from that of the wind.

Letter to Mersenne, Mar., 1636. I, 341.

SPACE

As for the question of whether there would be a real space, as there is now, in case God had created nothing, even though such a question exceeds the limits of the human mind, and is not something that can be reasonably debated, like questions concerning the infinite, nevertheless I believe that it does not exceed the bounds of our imagination, like questions of the existence of God and of the human soul, and that our understanding can attain the truth about them, which is, at least in my opinion, that not only would there be no space, but even the truths which are called eternal, like *the whole is greater than its parts,* etc., would not be truths, if God had not established them in that way.

Letter to Mersenne, May 17, 1638. II, 138.

❖ ❖ ❖

Space or interior place does not differ from the body which is comprised in that space, except by our thought.

Principles, II, 10. IX2, 68.

❖ ❖ ❖

We never distinguish space from extension in length, breadth and depth; but we sometimes consider the place as if it were in the thing which is placed, and sometimes also as if it were external to it. The interior does not differ from the space, but we sometimes take the exterior, either to be the surface which inmmediately surrounds the thing which is placed (and it is to be noted that, for the surface, one ought not to understand any part of the body which surrounds it, but only the extremity which is between the body which surrounds and that which is surrounded, which is nothing but a mode or an aspect), or to be the surface in general, which is not part of one body rather than another, and which seems always the same, as long as it is the same size and shape.

Principles, II, 15. IX2, 71.

SPACES, IMAGINARY

Supposing the world finite, one imagines beyond these limits some spaces which have their three dimensions, and thus which are not purely imaginary, as the philosophers call them.

Letter to Chanut, June 6, 1647. V, 52.

SPEECH

Speech is the unique sign and the sole assured mark of the thought which is hidden in the body; but all men, the most stupid and insane, even those who are deprived of the organs of language and speech, make use of signs, while the beasts do nothing similar, so that speech may be taken as the true difference between man and beast.

Letter to More, Feb. 5, 1649. V, 278.

SPIRITS

The more lively and subtle particles, that is, those which are quite fine, and together very solid and agitated, I will always henceforth call *spirits*.

Description of Human Body, IV. XI, 260.

❖   ❖   ❖

What I here call [animal] spirits are only bodies, and they have no other property than that of being very small, and moving very quickly, like the particles of flame which come from a torch.

Passions, I, 10. XI, 335.

SPIRITS, ANIMAL

As for the particles of blood which penetrate to the brain, they do not serve only to nourish and maintain its substance, but principally also to produce there a certain very subtle wind, or rather a very lively and very pure flame, which is called the *animal spirits*.

Treatise on Man. XI, 129.

◈ ◈ ◈

It is not the mind [or the soul] which immediately moves the external members [of our bodies], but it only determines the course of that very subtle liquid which is called the animal spirits, which, flowing continually from the heart through the brain into the muscles, is the cause of all the movements of our members.

Replies, IV. IX, 178.

◈ ◈ ◈

What [the doctors] call the animal spirits are nothing other than the most lively and subtle parts of the blood, which are separated from the grosser parts, as they are sifted out in the tiny branches of the carotid arteries, and which pass from there into the brain, from which they are distributed by the nerves into all the muscles.

Letter to Newcastle, Apr., 1645 (?). IV, 191.

◈ ◈ ◈

The most agitated and lively particles of the blood, when they are carried to the brain by the arteries that come from the heart most directly of all, compose an air or a very subtle wind, which is called the *animal spirits*; which, dilating the brain, render it proper to receive the impressions of external objects, and also those of the soul, that is to say, to be the organ or the seat of the *common sense, imagination*, and *memory*.

Description of Human Body, I. XI, 227.

SPIRITS, VITAL

What the doctors call the vital spirits are nothing other than the blood contained in the arteries, which does not differ from that of the veins, except in that it is rarer and warmer, because it has just been warmed and dilated in the heart.

Letter to Newcastle, Apr., 1645 (?). IV, 191.

210

SPRING WATER

Water is always similar to water, but it has quite another taste when one drinks it at the spring, than when he drinks it from a jug or from a stream.

To Beeckman, Oct. 17, 1630. I, 160.

STARS

It is quite likely that the surfaces of the skies, which are composed of a very fluid material, and which never stop moving, must always tremble and form waves somewhat; and, as a consequence, the stars that one sees through them must appear twinkling and as though trembling.

The World, XV. XI, 108.

STIFF

The property of bending and springing back, which can be briefly called being stiff, is generally found in all bodies of which the particles are joined by the perfect contact of their little surfaces, simply by the interlacing of their branches.

Principles, IV, 132. IX2, 270.

❖   ❖   ❖

See *flint*.

SUBSTANCE

Everything in which there resides immediately, as in its subject, or by which there exists, something that we conceive, i.e., some property, quality, or attribute, of which we have in us a real idea, is called *Substance*. For we do not have any other idea of substance in a precise sense, except that it is a thing in which there exists formally, or eminently, that which we conceive, or what is objectively in one of our ideas, inasmuch as the natural light teaches us that nothing can have no real attribute.

Replies, II. IX, 125.

❖   ❖   ❖

From the fact that we perceive some forms, or attributes, which must be attached to something if they are to exist, we

211

call by the name *Substance* that thing to which they are attached.

Replies, IV. IX, 172-173.

❖ ❖ ❖

We know a thing or substance better when we notice more properties in it.

Principles, I, 11. IX2, 29.

❖ ❖ ❖

When we conceive substance, we conceive only a thing which exists in such a way that it has no need of anything but itself for existence. In this, there could be some obscurity concerning the explanation of the phrase, "has no need of anything but itself"; for, properly speaking, only God is thus, and there is no created thing which could exist a single moment without being sustained and conserved by his power. This is why the School is correct in saying that the word substance is not "univocal" with regard to God and creatures, that is, that there is no signification in this word which we conceive distinctly, which applies to him and to them; but because among the created things some are of such a nature that they cannot exist without some others, we distinguish them from those which have no need other than the ordinary concurrence of God, and we call these substances, and the others the qualities or attributes of these substances.

Principles, I, 51. IX2, 47.

❖ ❖ ❖

Those [ideas] which represent substances to me are doubtless something more, and contain in themselves (so to speak) more objective reality, i.e., participate by representation in more degrees of being or perfection, than those which represent only modes or accidents.

Meditations, III. IX, 31-32,

SUN

The rays of the Sun have a most remarkable advantage in comparison with those of a torch: which is that their force does not diminish, and even increases more and more, as they are farther and farther from the Sun.

The World, XV. XI, 109.

❖   ❖   ❖

We may believe that the sun is composed of matter which is quite liquid, the particles of which are extremely agitated, so that they carry with them the particles of the sky in the vicinity of the sun and which surround them; but, in common with the fixed stars, the sun does not pass from one part of the sky to another.

Principles, III, 21. IX2, 111.

❖   ❖   ❖

The sun has no need of fuel, as does flame.

Principles, III, 22. IX2, 111.

SUNSPOTS

You do not tell me which side the poles are on, of the band along which the sunspots have been seen, but I do not doubt that they correspond in some way to those of the earth, and their ecliptic to our own.

Letter to Mersenne, Mar. 4, 1630. I, 125.

❖   ❖   ❖

Let us think also that the opaque bodies which are seen with telescopes upon the sun, and which are named its spots, move over its surface, and take twenty-six days to complete their revolution.

Principles, III, 32. IX2, 116.

SUPERSTITION

It is good to have examined all sciences, even the most superstitious and false, in order to know their value and to guard oneself against being deceived.

Discourse, I. VI, 6.

See *number; astrology.*

SUPPOSITIONS

If some of the things about which I have spoken, at the

213

beginning of the *Dioptrics* and the *Meteorology* are surprising at first, because I call them suppositions, and do not seem to have any desire to prove them, one should have enough patience to read the whole with attention, and I hope that he will find himself satisfied with it.

Discourse, VI. VI, 76.

❖   ❖   ❖

I imitate the astronomers, who, even though their suppositions are almost all false or uncertain, nevertheless, because they are connected with various observations that they have made, can derive many consequences from them which are quite true and quite assured.

Discourse, VI. VI, 83.

❖   ❖   ❖

It is to be noted that although I speak of suppositions, I nevertheless do not make any [here] whose falsehood, even though it is well known, can give occasion for doubting the truth of the conclusions which are derived from them.

Principles, III, 47. IX2, 126.

SURFACE

There is no other thing by which our senses are touched, except the surface which is the limit of the dimensions of the body which is sensed or perceived by the senses.

Replies, IV. IX, 192.

❖   ❖   ❖

The word surface is taken in two ways by the mathematicians: namely, either for the body of which only the length and breadth are being considered, without regard to its depth, even though it is not denied that there is one; or it is taken solely as a mode of body, and then all depth is denied to it.

Replies, VI. IX, 234.

❖   ❖   ❖

By the word surface, I do not understand some substance of real nature which could be destroyed by the omnipotence of God, but solely a mode or a fashion of being, which cannot be changed without changing that in which or by which it exists; as it implies a contradiction to say that the square shape of a piece of wax is taken from it and that nevertheless none of the parts of the wax change their places.

Letter to Mesland, Feb. 9, 1644. IV, 163-164.

◈　◈　◈

See *space; identity.*

SURPRISE

[Wonder has] a great deal of force, because of surprise, that is, the sudden and unexpected arrival of the impression which changes the motion of the [animal] spirits; this surprise is proper and particular to that passion.

Passions, II, 72. XI, 381.

SYLLOGISMS

The dialecticians cannot construct anything according to the rules of the syllogism, which will have a true conclusion, if they do not already have the material for it, that is, if they do not know in advance that same truth which they are deriving.

Rules, X. X, 406.

SYLLOGISMS, PROBABLE

We do not condemn that method of philosophizing which others have already discovered and those weapons of the schoolmen, probable syllogisms, which are so well suited for polemics. They indeed give practice to the wits of youths and, producing emulation among them, act as a stimulus; and it is much better for their minds to be moulded by opinions of this sort, uncertain though they appear, as being objects of controversy among the learned, than to be left entirely to their own devices.

Rules, II. X, 363-364.

SYNTHESIS

Synthesis follows a path quite different [from that of analysis], as though it were examining causes by their effects (even though the proof that it contains is often also of effects by their causes), and truly demonstrates what is contained in its

215

conclusions, and serves as a long sequence of definitions, presuppositions, axioms, theorems, and problems, so that, if some consequences are denied, it shows how they are contained in their antecedents, and how it forces the consent of the reader, however obstinate and opinionated he might be; but it does not give, as does analysis, a complete satisfaction to the minds of those who desire to learn, because it does not teach the method by which the subject has been invented.

Replies, II. IX, 122.

See *analysis*.

T

TABLET, BLANK

One [may] compare the imagination of children to a blank tablet, upon which our ideas are to be placed, which are like portraits drawn from each thing as it is. Sense, inclination, teachers, and the understanding are the different painters who can labor at this work; among them, the least capable are the first to have a hand in it, namely the imperfect senses, blind instincts, and impertinent appetites.

Search for Truth. X, 508.

TANGENT

The angle which a straight line makes with a curved line to which it is tangent, is smaller than any angle which could be made by two straight lines, and of all the curved lines, there is only the circle which has the tangent angle always equal at every point.

Principles, IV, 19. IX2, 210.

TASTE

The tiny threads which compose the marrow of the nerves of the tongue, and which serve as organs of *taste* in this machine [the body], can be moved by smaller actions than those which might serve for the sense of touch in general.

Treatise on Man. XI, 145.

❖　　❖　　❖

The sense which is grossest, after touch, is taste, which has as its organ the nerves of the tongue and of the other parts which surround it, and as its object the tiny particles of earthly bodies which, when they are separated from one another, swim in the saliva which moistens the interior of the mouth: for, according to whether they are different in shape, in size, or in motion, they cause different movements in the tips of these nerves and by means of them make the soul sense all sorts of different tastes.

Principles, IV, 192. IX2, 313.

TASTES

There are as many different tastes as there are ways in which the nerves of the tongue are differently affected. There are nine possibilities: insipid or mild, rich, sweet, bitter, hot, acid, salt, acrid, and sour.

On Tastes. XI, 539.

TEARS

Love joined to sadness causes most tears.

Passions, II, 117. XI, 415.

❖   ❖   ❖

Just as laughter is never caused by the greatest joys, so also tears do not come from extreme sadness, but only from a sadness which is mediocre and accompanied or followed by some sensation of love, or also of joy.

Passions, II, 128. XI, 422-423.

TEND

When I say that a body tends toward one side, I do not wish anyone to imagine that there is a thought or a will in it, which moves it, but only that it is disposed to move in that direction: either it actually moves, or some other body prevents it from moving; and it is principally in this latter sense that I make use of the word *to tend,* because it seems to signify some effort, and every effort presupposes some resistance.

The World, XIII. XI, 84.

❖   ❖   ❖

Since it often happens that a variety of different causes, acting together upon the same body, impede the effect of one another, one can say, according to various considerations, that the body tends, or makes an effort, to go in various directions at the same time.

Principles, III, 57. IX2, 131.

TENDENCY

See *inclination.*

THEOLOGY

Theology is so dominated by Aristotle that it is almost impossible to discuss another philosophy without its immediately seeming contrary to Faith.

Letter to Mersenne, Dec. 18, 1629. I, 85-86.

❖   ❖   ❖

I do not think that there will be any difficulty in accommodating theology to my way of philosophizing; for I do not see anything to change in theology except for transsubstantiation, which is extremely clear and easy by my principles.

Letter to Mersenne, Jan. 28, 1641. III, 295-296.

❖   ❖   ❖

I have never made a profession of the study of theology, and I have never applied myself to it except as much as I thought necessary for my own instruction, and, finally, I do not sense any divine inspiration in me which would make me judge myself capable of teaching it.

Replies, VI. IX, 230.

❖   ❖   ❖

We ought to demonstrate that the truths of theology are not opposed to the truths of philosophy, but we ought not in any manner to criticize them.

Burman. V, 176.

❖   ❖   ❖

Simple persons and rustics can gain heaven as well as we can. That certainly ought to warn us that it is better to have a theology as simple as theirs, than to torment it by so many controversies, to corrupt it in this way, and to give birth to disputes, quarrels, wars, etc., especially since the theologians have acquired the habit of lending all their opinions to the theologians of the opposite party, of slandering them, to the point of rendering the art of slander so familiar that they can hardly do anything other than slander, even on their own side.

Burman. V, 176.

THING

I deny flatly that we do not know what a "thing" is, or what a "thought" is, or that there is any need for me to teach others what these are, because all these are so manifest in themselves that there is nothing by which they could be explained more clearly.

Letter to "Hyperaspistas," Aug., 1641. III, 426.

THINGS IN THEMSELVES

Things in themselves can be considered only insofar as they are accessible to the understanding.

Rules, VIII. X, 399.

THINKING

Willing, understanding, imagining, sensing, etc., are only various ways of thinking, and all of them belong to the soul.

Letter to Mersenne, May, 1637. I, 366.

THINKING THING

What is a thinking thing? It is a thing which doubts, conceives, affirms, denies, wills, refuses, imagines, and senses.

Meditations, II. IX, 22.

❖   ❖   ❖

I am a thinking thing, that is, who doubt, affirm, deny, know a few things, am ignorant of many, love, hate, will, refuse, imagine, and sense.

Meditations, III. IX, 27.

❖   ❖   ❖

My essence consists in this alone, that I am a thinking thing, or a substance whose whole essence or nature is to think.

Meditations, VI. IX, 62.

THOUGHTS

There is nothing completely in our power other than our thoughts.

Discourse, III. VI, 25.

In one sense, I include images in the definition of *cogitatio,* or thought, and in another sense I exclude them, as follows: The forms or corporeal species which must exist in the brain for us to imagine something, are not thoughts, but the operation of the mind which imagines, i.e., which turns toward these species, is a thought.

Letter to Mersenne, Apr. 21, 1641. III, 361.

◈   ◈   ◈

Among my thoughts, some are like images of things, and it is these alone which are properly called "ideas": as when I represent to myself a man, or a chimera, or the heavens, or an angel, or God himself. Others, besides these, have some other forms: as, when I will, when I fear, when I affirm or when I deny, I then conceive something as the subject of the action of my mind, but I also add some other thing by that action to the idea that I have of that thing; and of this type of thought, the first are called volitions, or affections, and the others judgments.

Meditations, III. IX, 29.

◈   ◈   ◈

Our soul is of such a nature that the movements which take place in the body are sufficient to make it have all sorts of thoughts, without the necessity of there being anything in them which resembles what they make the soul conceive; and, in particular, they can excite in the soul those confused thoughts which are called the sensations.

Principles, IV, 197. IX2, 315.

◈   ◈   ◈

Our soul, insofar as it is a substance which is distinct from the body, is not known to us except by the sole fact that it thinks, that is, that it understands, wills, imagines, recollects, and senses, because all these functions are species of thoughts.

Description of Human Body, I. XI, 224.

❖   ❖   ❖

There is nothing in us which we ought to attribute to our soul, other than our thoughts, which are principally of two types: some are the actions of the soul, others are passions. Those which I call its actions are all our acts of will, because we experience the fact that they come directly from our soul and seem to depend only on it. On the other hand, one can call passions all the kinds of perceptions or knowledge which are found in us, because it is not often that our soul makes them what they are, and because the soul always receives them from things which are represented by these thoughts.

Passions, I, 17. XI, 342.

❖   ❖   ❖

I use the word "thought" for all the operations of the soul, in such a way that not only meditations and volitions but even the functions of seeing, hearing, determining oneself to one movement rather than to another, etc., insofar as they depend on us, are thoughts.

Letter to Reneri, Apr.-May, 1638. II, 36.

❖   ❖   ❖

When the mind is united to the body and thinks of something corporeal, certain particles of the brain are moved from their places, sometimes by the external objects which act upon the sense organs, and sometimes by the animal spirits which rise from the heart to the brain; but sometimes also by the mind itself, namely when, of itself and by its own freedom, it turns to a certain thought.

Letter to "Hyperaspistas," Aug., 1641. III, 425.

❖   ❖   ❖

I find that thought is an attribute which belongs to me: it alone cannot be detached from me.

Meditations, II. IX, 21.

❖   ❖   ❖

By the word *thought* I understand all that is in us in such a way that we know it immediately. Thus all the operations of the will, understanding, imagination and senses are thoughts.

But I have added *immediately* to exclude the things which follow and depend upon our thoughts: for example, voluntary motion certainly has the will as its principle, but it itself is nevertheless not a thought.

Replies, II. IX, 124.

❖   ❖   ❖

It is certain that thought cannot be without a thing which thinks, and in general no accident or act can be without a substance of which it is the act.

Replies, III. IX, 136.

❖   ❖   ❖

We see very well that there is nothing in [the mind], when it is considered [as a thinking thing], which is not a thought, or which does not depend entirely upon thought: otherwise it would not pertain to the mind, insofar as it is a thinking thing; and there can be no thought in us of which, in the same moment that it is in us, we do not have actual knowledge.

Replies, IV. IX, 190.

❖   ❖   ❖

Having an idea or notion of thought which is completely different from that of motion, one must necessarily conceive one as different from the other.

Replies, VI. IX, 226.

❖   ❖   ❖

To apprehend what doubt is, or what thought is, it is necessary only to doubt and think.

Search for Truth. X, 525.

❖   ❖   ❖

By the word thought, I understand everything that takes place within us of such a sort that we perceive it immediately by ourselves; this is why not only understanding, willing, imagining, but also sensing, is the same thing here as thinking.

Principles, I, 9. IX2. 28.

See *thing*.

THOUGHT, DIRECT AND REFLECTIVE

As we make a distinction between direct and reflected vision, in that the former depends on the first encounter of the light and the latter on the second; so I call the first and simple thoughts of [unborn] infants those which arrive, for example, when they sense pain because of some gas enclosed in their bowels which makes them expand, or pleasure from the fact that the blood by which they are nourished is sweet; I call these *direct* and non-reflective: but when a young man senses something new, and when at the same time he perceives that he has not sensed the same thing previously, I call that second perception a *reflection*, and I refer it solely to the understanding, even though it is so conjoined with the sensation that they take place together, and do not seem to be distinguished from one another.

Letter to Arnauld, July 29, 1648. V, 220-221.

THUNDER

From the fact alone that the particles of the upper clouds fall altogether or one after the other, either faster or more slowly, and from the fact that the lower clouds are larger or smaller, thicker or thinner, and resist more or less, all the different sounds of thunder may easily be caused.

Meteorology, VII. VI, 317.

TICKLING

If they [the threads at the center of the nerves] are pulled with a force almost as great as the preceding [which causes pain], without being broken, nor being separated in any way from the particles to which they are attached: they will cause a movement in the brain, which, bearing witness to the good constitution of the other members, will give occasion to the soul to sense a certain corporeal pleasure, which is called *tickling*, and which, as you see, is quite close to pain in its cause, but which is completely contrary in its effect.

Treatise on Man. XI, 144.

TIME

Actually, it is very clear and evident [to everyone who considers the nature of time attentively] that a substance has need of the same action and the same power if it is to be conserved

.during all the moments that it lasts, that would be necessary to produce and create it again, if it did not previously exist.

Meditations, III. IX, 39.

◈   ◈   ◈

The parts of time can be separated from one another, and thus, from the fact that I am now, it does not follow that I must be at a later time, if, so to speak, I am not created anew at each moment by some cause.

Replies, I. IX, 86.

◈   ◈   ◈

The present time does not depend upon that which has immediately preceded it.

Replies, II. IX, 127.

◈   ◈   ◈

In order to comprehend the duration of all things under the same measure, we ordinarily make use of the duration of certain regular movements, which are the days, and the years, and we call it *time*, after having compared these motions with others; even though, in actuality, what we call time is nothing but a way of thinking, aside from the true duration of things.

Principles, I, 57. IX2. 50.

◈   ◈   ◈

There is no time imaginable, before the creation of the world, at which God could have created it, if he had wished.

Letter to Chanut, June 6, 1647. V, 52.

TOP

Just as we see that a [child's] top acquires enough force, simply by being set in motion by a child's turning it between his fingers, to continue afterward by itself for several minutes, and make perhaps more than two or three thousand turns about its center during this time, even though it is quite small, and even though so much of the air which surrounds it and the earth which holds it up resist this motion and retard it with all their power: one can easily believe that, if a planet had been set in motion in the same way at the time it was created, that alone would be enough for it to continue

225

the same motion, without any notable diminution, until the present time, because, the bigger a body is, the more it can retain for a longer time the motion which has been impressed upon it, and because the period of five or six thousand years that the world has existed, if it is compared with the size of a planet, is not as much as a minute compared with the smallness of a top.

Principles, III, 144. IX2, 193.

TOUCH

Touch is believed to be the least deceptive and the most assured of all our senses.

The World, I. XI, 5.

❖   ❖   ❖

The first [external sense] is touch, which has as its object all the bodies which can move some part of the flesh or the skin of our body, and as its organs all the nerves which, being found in that part of our body, participate in its movement.

Principles, IV, 191. IX2, 312.

TRAGEDY

Even elegies and tragedies please us all the more, the more they excite compassion and sadness in us, and the more they touch us.

Compendium Musicae. X, 89.

TRANQUILITY

As for me, I seek only repose and tranquility of mind, which are goods which cannot be possessed by those who have animosity or ambition.

Letter to Mersenne, Feb., 1634. I, 282.

TREE OF PORPHYRY

If to explain what an animal is, he [Epistemon] replies that it is a living and sensitive being, and that a living being is an animate body, and that a body is a corporeal substance; you see immediately that the questions go on, growing and multiplying like the branches of a genealogical tree [i.e., the tree of Porphyry], and it is quite evident that all these beautiful questions end in a pure tautology which clarifies nothing and leaves us in our original ignorance.

Search for Truth. X, 516.

TREMBLING

Trembling has two different causes: one is that sometimes too few spirits come from the brain into the nerves, and the other that sometimes too many come there.

Passions, II, 118. XI, 415.

TRINITY

Concerning the mystery of the Trinity, I judge, with St. Thomas, that it is purely a matter of faith, and cannot be known by the natural light.

Letter to Mersenne, Dec. 31, 1640. III, 274.

TRUE

I do not know whether these [ideas] are true, or false and simply apparent, i.e., if the ideas that I conceive of these qualities are actually the ideas of some real things, or if they only represent chimerical beings to me, which could not exist.

Meditations, III. IX, 34.

❖   ❖   ❖

It is very evident that everything which is true is something and I have already amply demonstrated that everything that I know clearly and distinctly is true.

Meditations, V. IX, 51-52.

❖   ❖   ❖

I wish to have it thought that if what I have written about that [the circulation of the blood], or about refraction, or about any other subject that I have treated in more than three lines in what I have had printed, is found to be false, then all the rest of my philosophy is worthless.

Letter to Mersenne, Feb. 9, 1639. II, 501.

❖   ❖   ❖

I neither pretend nor promise in any way that everything that I have written is true.

Letter to Chanut, June 15, 1646. IV, 441.

227

TRUTH

It seemed to me that I would be able to find much more truth in the reasoning of each person concerning the affairs that are important to him, the results of which will punish him soon afterward, if he has judged badly, than in the reasoning of a man of letters in his study, concerning speculations which produce no effect whatever.

Discourse, I. VI, 9-10.

❖ ❖ ❖

The word *truth*, in its proper signification, denotes the conformity of the thought with the object, but when it is attributed to things which are external to thought, it signifies only that these things can serve as objects of true thoughts, either ours or those of God.

Letter to Mersenne, Oct. 16, 1639. II, 597.

❖ ❖ ❖

I ought not in any way to doubt the truth of these things [my waking experiences], if after having called all my senses, my memory and my understanding to examine them, nothing is reported to me by any of them which conflicts with what is reported to me by the others.

Meditations, VI. IX, 71-72.

❖ ❖ ❖

It is certain that to find [the truth] one ought always to begin with particular notions, in order later to go on to general notions, even though he may also, conversely, having found general notions, deduce other particulars from them.

Letter to Clerselier. IX, 206.

TRUTHS, CONTINGENT

As for contingent truths [like "the dog runs"], they concern the existing things that they involve, as they are involved by them.

Burman. V, 167.

TRUTHS, ETERNAL

The mathematical truths, which you call eternal, have been established by God and depend on him entirely, like all the other creatures.

Letter to Mersenne, Apr. 15, 1630. I, 145.

❖ ❖ ❖

As for the eternal truths, I say again that they are true or possible simply because God knows them as true or possible; but, on the other hand, I do not say that they are known by God as true in the sense that truths exist independently of him.

Letter to Mersenne, May 6, 1630. I, 149.

❖ ❖ ❖

I will content myself with pointing out to you that, other than the three laws that I have explained, I do not want to assume any other laws, except those which follow infallibly from these eternal truths, upon which mathematicians are accustomed to base their most certain and most evident demonstrations: the truths, I say, following which God himself has taught us that he has disposed everything in number, in weight, and in measure; and of which the knowledge is so natural to our souls, that we cannot fail to judge that they are infallible, when we conceive them distinctly, nor to doubt that, if God had created many worlds, these truths would be as true in all of them as they are in this world.

The World, VII. XI, 47.

❖ ❖ ❖

One must not think that the eternal truths depend upon the human understanding, or upon the existence of things, but solely upon the will of God, who, like a sovereign legislator, has ordained and established them for all eternity.

Replies, IV. IX, 236.

❖ ❖ ❖

See *laws; space.*

U

UNDERSTANDING

A man who proposes to himself the problem of examining all the truths for the knowledge of which human reason suffices— an examination that all those who seriously intend to raise themselves to the level of good sense ought to make once in their lives—will certainly find, according to the rules which have been given, that one can know nothing before he knows the understanding [or intellect], because the knowledge of everything else depends on it, and not conversely.

Rules, VIII. X, 395.

❖   ❖   ❖

Only the understanding is capable of perceiving truth.

Rules, XII. X, 411.

❖   ❖   ❖

Understanding [*intellectio*] is properly a passion of the soul, and the act of will its action.

Letter to Regius, May, 1641. III, 372.

❖   ❖   ❖

Properly speaking, we do not conceive bodies except by the faculty of understanding, which is in us, and not by the imagination or by the senses, and we do not know them from what we see or what we touch, but solely by what we conceive with thought.

Meditations, II. IX, 26.

❖   ❖   ❖

Even bodies are not properly known by the senses, but by the understanding alone.

Replies, II. IX, 105.

❖   ❖   ❖

I do not say that intellection and the thing which understands are the same thing, nor even that the thing which understands

231

and the understanding are the same, if understanding is taken as a faculty, but only when it is taken as the thing itself which understands.

Replies, III. IX, 135.

❖　❖　❖

We must distinguish with care among understanding, conceiving, and imagining: a distinction which is of great use, for example [concerning], the perfections of God; we do not imagine them, nor conceive them, but we understand them.

Burman. V, 154.

UNITY

Unity is that common nature in which everything that we compare ought to participate equally.

Rules, XIV. X, 449.

UNIVERSALS

Universals arise solely from the fact that we use the same idea for thinking of many particular things which have a certain similarity among themselves. And when we comprehend the things which are represented by that idea under the same name, that name is also universal.

Principles, I, 59. IX2, 50.

❖　❖　❖

Ordinarily five universals are counted: genus, species, difference, property, and accident.

Principles, I, 59. IX2, 51.

❖　❖　❖

See *number.*

USAGE

It seems to me that it is only the general public, to whom one ought to give the right to authorize, by long usage, the names which they have improperly imposed upon things; and because the public do not customarily speak about this [i.e., the naming of the north and south poles of the magnet], but only those who philosophize, and desire to know the truth, I am sure that they will not find it wrong of me to prefer reason to [their] usage.

Principles, IV, 149. IX2, 285.

V

VACUUM

See *void*.

VAPORS

These tiny particles, which are thus raised up in the air by the sun, ought for the most part to have the shape that I have attributed to those of water, because there are no others which can so easily be separated from the bodies to which they belong; and it is these alone which I will call *vapors,* in particular, in order to distinguish them from others which have more irregular shapes, and to which I will restrict the name *exhalation,* because I know of no better name for them.

Meteorology, II. VI, 240.

VENERATION

When we esteem or scorn other objects, which we consider as free causes, capable of doing good or evil, from esteem comes veneration, and from scorn, disdain.

Passions, II, 55. XI, 374.

❖   ❖   ❖

Veneration or respect is an inclination of the soul, not only to esteem the object that it reveres, but also to submit to it with some fear, in the attempt to render it favorable to oneself.

Passions, III, 162. XI, 454.

VENGEANCE

Just as, in order to straighten a bent stick, we bend it, not merely until it is straight, but until it bends in the opposite direction, similarly, because our nature is too much inclined to vengeance, God does not command us merely to pardon our enemies, but even to do good to them.

Letter to Mersenne, Jan., 1630. I, 110.

233

VICES

I call vices the sicknesses of the soul. They are less easy to recognize than the sicknesses of the body, because we have often experienced good health in the body, but never in the soul.

Cogitationes Privatae. X, 215.

◈ ◈ ◈

As all the vices come only from the uncertainty and weakness which follows ignorance, and which generates repentance; so also virtue consists only in the resolution and vigor with which one tends to do the things that he believes to be good, provided that that vigor does not come from obstinacy, but from knowing that he has examined things as much as he morally can.

Letter to Christine, Nov. 20, 1647. V, 83-84.

VICTORY

[Victory:] Although this court is filled with ladies, who cannot be too much esteemed, and whom the noblest souls are obliged to love; I still surpass the most beautiful of them in beauty. And the proof of this is that for one lover who sighs for them, a thousand die for me.

Birth of Peace, VI.

VIOLENCE

The word violence is applied only to our will, which is said to suffer violence when something is done which is repellent to it; thus in nature there is no violence, but it is as natural to bodies to clash against one another, or to break into pieces when that happens, as to remain at rest.

Letter to More, Aug., 1649. V, 404.

VIRTUE

[Zeno the Stoic] represented virtue as so severe and so much an enemy of pleasure, making all the vices equal, that it seems to me that it was only melancholics, or minds entirely detached from bodies, who could have been members of his sect.

Letter to Elisabeth, Aug. 18, 1645. IV, 276.

◈ ◈ ◈

It is certain that one cannot have too ardent a desire for virtue.

Passions, II, 144. XI, 437.

234

Whoever has lived in such a way that his conscience cannot accuse him even of failing to do all the things which he has judged to be the best (which is what I call following the path of virtue), he receives a satisfaction from it, which is so capable of making him happy, that the most violent efforts of the passions never have enough power to trouble the tranquility of his soul.

Passions, II, 148. XI, 442.

See *vice*.

VOICE, HUMAN

And it seems that what makes the human voice more agreeable to us than other sounds is simply that it better conforms to the nature of our spirits. Perhaps it is also the sympathy or antipathy of humor and inclination that makes the voice of a friend seem more agreeable to us than that of an enemy, for the same reason that it is said that a drum covered with lambskin no longer resounds, and loses its sound entirely, after one has beaten on another drum covered with wolfskin.

Compendium Musicae. X, 90.

VOID

There is no void, as I believe that I can demonstrate.

Letter to Mersenne, April 15, 1630. I, 140.

◈　◈　◈

When the wine in a barrel fails to flow out of the opening at the bottom of the barrel, because the top is completely sealed, it is improper to say, as one does ordinarily, that this is due to "fear of the void." Everyone knows that the wine has no mind with which it can fear something, and even if it did, I do not know why it should fear the void, which is actually nothing but a chimera.

The World, IV. XI, 20.

◈　◈　◈

There is no void in Nature.

The World, IV. XI, 20.

◈　◈　◈

What he [Galileo] attributes to the void should only be attributed to the weight of the air; and it is certain that, if it was the fear of the void which kept two bodies from being separated, there would be no force which could separate them.

Letter to Mersenne, Oct. 11, 1638. II, 382.

◈　◈　◈

I attribute nothing to "void" nor to "fear of the void."

Letter to Mersenne, Oct. 11, 1638. II, 399.

◈　◈　◈

As for the void, in the sense in which the philosophers take the word, that is, as a space where there is no substance, it is evident that there is no such space anywhere in the universe, because the extension of space, or interior place, is no different from the extension of body.

Principles, II, 16. IX2, 71.

◈　◈　◈

When we take the word according to ordinary usage and say that a place is void, it is an established fact that we do not wish to say that there is nothing at all in that place or in that space, but only that there is nothing that we presume ought to be there.

Principles, II, 17. IX2, 72.

◈　◈　◈

[Possibly] all the space which is around the earth, and is not filled with any of the earth's particles, is void, that is, it is not filled with any body which could aid or impede the motions of other bodies (for that is what we ought properly to understand by the word void).

Principles, IV, 21. IX2, 210-211.

◈　◈　◈

It implies a contradiction for there to be a void, because we have the same idea of matter as of space; and because that idea represents a real thing to us, we contradict ourselves, and affirm the contrary of what we think if we say that that space is void, that is, that what we conceive as a real thing is nothing real.

Letter to Newcastle, Oct., 1645. IV, 329.

VORTEX

Let us think that the matter of the sky, where the planets are, turns continuously around, like a vortex which has the sun at its center.

Principles, III, 30. IX2, 115.

❖   ❖   ❖

As in the bends of the rivers where the water flows back upon itself, and thus turning, makes circles, if some straws or other very light bodies are floating in the water, one can see that it carries them along and makes them move around with it; and even, among these straws, one can notice that there are often some which turn about their own centers; and that those which are closest to the center of the vortex which contains them complete their turning sooner than those which are farther from it; and finally that, even though these vortices of water always turn around, they almost never describe circles which are entirely perfect, and they are sometimes longer, sometimes broader, in such a way that all the parts of the circumference that they describe are not equally distant from the center. Thus one can easily imagine that the same things happen to the planets; and this is all that is needed to explain all their phenomena.

Principles, III, 30. IX2, 115-116.

❖   ❖   ❖

I will henceforth use this word [vortex] to signify all the matter which turns in this way about each of these centers [i.e., about the stars, planets, and other centers].

Principles, III, 46. IX2, 125.

W

WAR

The best possible war always destroys the beauties of the earth, and the greatest of its benefits comes when it gives us peace.

Birth of Peace, Prologue.

❖ ❖ ❖

[War:] I crush the boulders, I level the mountains, I destroy the ditches, I mine the castles, I cover the seas with blood, I burn the ships, and I strew the most beautiful fields with dead men's bodies.

Birth of Peace, I.

❖ ❖ ❖

[Soldiers, crippled in the war:] Anyone who sees what has happened to us and thinks that war is beautiful, or that it is worth more than peace, is crippled in the brain.

Birth of Peace, VII.

❖ ❖ ❖

It must be confessed that no one can find war good; that all its fruits are bitter; and that peace must be desired.

Birth of Peace, VIII.

WATER

If water is more fluid, and if it does not solidify as easily as oil, this is an indication that the oil is composed of particles which are easily joined one to the other, as are the branches of trees, and that water is composed of particles which are more slippery, as are those of the shape of eels.

Letter to Plempius, Oct. 3, 1637. I, 423.

As for water, I have already shown how it is composed of two sorts of particles, which are quite long and smooth, of which some are soft and flexible, and the others are stiff and inflexible, in such a way that, when they are separated, the latter are the components of salt, and the former of sweet water.

Principles, I, 48. IX2, 48.

WEAK MINDEDNESS

No one is so weak minded that he cannot comprehend that, when he is sitting, he differs in a certain sense from himself when he is standing up.

Rules, XII. X, 425.

WEIGHT

The weight of the particles of the Earth is caused by the action of the matter of the Sky, which is in its pores.

The World, XII. XI, 80.

◈ ◈ ◈

The weight of the Earth, that is, the force which unites all its parts and which makes them tend toward its center, each one more or less, according as they are more or less gross and solid; the weight is nothing more and consists only in the fact that the particles of the small Sky which surrounds it, turning much more quickly than the Earth's particles about their center, tend also with more force to retard it and, as a consequence, to repel it.

The World, XI. XI, 72-73.

◈ ◈ ◈

I do not believe that heavy bodies fall by some *real quality*, named *weight*, such as the philosophers imagine, nor because of some attraction of the earth.

Letter to Mersenne, June or July, 1635. I, 324.

◈ ◈ ◈

Concerning weight, I imagine nothing else than that all the subtle matter which is between here and the moon, turning very rapidly about the earth, drives all the bodies which cannot move so rapidly toward the earth.

Letter to Debeaune, Apr. 30, 1639. II, 544.

❖   ❖   ❖

I say that [weight] comes from the fact that subtle matter, turning very rapidly about the earth, forces terrestrial bodies toward the center of its motion.

Letter to Mersenne, July 30, 1640. III, 134.

❖   ❖   ❖

I thought [as a child] that weight carried bodies toward the center of the earth, as if it had had in itself some knowledge of that center.

Replies, IV. IX, 240-241.

❖   ❖   ❖

[The quality of weight] is nothing really distinguished from body, as I hope to show in the *Physics* [i.e., *Principles of Philosophy*], but it has been given to us in order to conceive the way in which the soul moves the body.

Letter to Elisabeth, May 21, 1643. III, 667-668.

❖   ❖   ❖

The subtle matter, which, simply because of the fact that it moves in all directions indifferently about a drop of water, impels all parts of its surface equally toward its center, and [in the same way] simply because it moves about the earth, it also impels toward the earth all the bodies which are said to have weight, which are its parts.

Principles, IV, 20. IX2, 210.

❖   ❖   ❖

Most philosophers who believe that the weight of a stone is a real quality, distinct from the stone, believe that they understand quite well in what way that quality can move a stone toward the center of the earth, because they believe that they have had a manifest experience of it: as for me, who persuade myself that there is no such quality in nature, and as a consequence that there could not be any true idea of it in the human understanding, I believe that they make use of the idea which they have in themselves of incorporeal substance to represent that weight.

Letter to Arnauld, July 29, 1648. V, 223.

241

WILL

Our will naturally desires only the things which our understanding represents to it as somehow possible.

Discourse, III. VI, 25-26.

❖ ❖ ❖

Because our will does not lead us to pursue or to avoid anything except according to whether our understanding represents it as good or bad, it is enough to judge well in order to do well.

Discourse, III. I, 28.

❖ ❖ ❖

This movement [enlargement of the pupil of the eye] ought to be called voluntary even though it is ordinarily not known by those who make it, because it is nonetheless dependent upon and follows from the will to see more clearly; just as the movements of the lips and the tongue, which serve for the pronunciation of words, are called voluntary, because they follow from the will to speak, even though one often does not know what movements should be used in the pronunciation of each letter.

Dioptrics, III. VI, 107-108.

❖ ❖ ❖

I claim that we have ideas not only of everything which is in our intellect, but even of everything which is in our will. For we would not know how to will anything, without knowing that we willed it, nor know it except by an idea; but I do not propose that that idea is different from the action itself.

Letter to Mersenne, Jan. 28, 1641. III, 295.

❖ ❖ ❖

The desire that everyone has to have all the perfections that he can conceive, and, as a consequence, all those which we believe to be in God, comes from the fact that God has given us a will which has no limits. And it is principally because of the infinite will which is in us that one can say that God has created us in his image.

Letter to Mersenne, Dec. 25, 1639. II, 628.

❖ ❖ ❖

The will does not comprehend, but only wills; and although it is true that we do not ever will anything in which we do not comprehend something, in some fashion, as I have previously conceded, nevertheless experience shows us well enough that we can will much more of a given thing than we can know of it.

Letter to "Hyperaspistas," Aug., 1641. III, 432.

❖ ❖ ❖

There is the will alone which I experience in myself to be so great that I do not conceive the idea of any other which is more ample and more extended: to the extent that it is principally the will which makes me know that I carry the image of and resemblance to God.

Meditations, IV. IX, 45.

❖ ❖ ❖

[The will] consists solely in the fact that we can do a thing or not do it (that is, affirm or deny, follow or flee), or rather simply in that, to affirm or deny, to follow or to flee, the things that the understanding proposes to us, we act in such a way that we do not sense that any external force constrains us to it.

Meditations, IV. IX, 46.

❖ ❖ ❖

The will turns voluntarily, and freely (for that is of its essence), but nevertheless infallibly, to the good which is clearly known to it.

Replies, II. IX, 128.

❖ ❖ ❖

Each person ought to look only within himself to discover there whether he does not have a perfect and absolute will, and whether he can conceive anything which restricts the freedom of his will. Assuredly, no one will have a different experience. It is in this that the will is greater than the understanding, and more similar to God.

Burman. V, 159.

♦ ♦ ♦

One may say that the will is corrupted by the effect of the passions.

Burman. V, 159.

♦ ♦ ♦

Acts of our will are of two sorts. Some are actions of the soul which terminate in the soul itself, as when we will to love God, or generally to apply our thought to some object which is not material. The others are actions which terminate in our body, as when, from the sole fact that we have the desire to take a walk, it follows that our limbs move and that we walk.

Passions, I, 18. XI, 342-343.

♦ ♦ ♦

The will is so free by nature, that it can never be constrained.

Passions, I, 41. XI, 359.

WILL, DIVINE

As for the freedom of the free will, it is certain that that which is found in God is quite different from that which is in us, inasmuch as it is contradictory to suppose that the will of God has not been, from all eternity, indifferent to all the things which have been done or which will ever be done, not having any idea which represents the good or the true, what must be believed, what must be done, or what must be omitted, which can be supposed to have been the object of the divine understanding, before its nature had been thus constituted by the determination of God's will.

Replies, VI. IX, 232-233.

WILL, FREE

As for free will, I confess that when we think only of ourselves, we cannot fail to think that it is free; but when we think of the infinite power of God, we cannot fail to believe that all things depend upon him, and, as a consequence, that our free will is not exempt.

Letter to Elisabeth, Nov. 3, 1645. IV, 332.

I do not see anything in us which can give us justification for self-esteem, other than the use of our free will, and our dominion over our acts of will. For it is only the actions which depend upon this free will, for which we can reasonably be praised or blamed; and it somehow makes us similar to God, since it makes us masters of ourselves, provided that we do not lose through cowardice the rights which it gives us.

Passions, III, 152. XI, 445.

WILLING

See *perception.*

WINDS

It is not only when the clouds dissolve in vapors that they cause the winds, but they can also sometimes fall so suddenly that they drive out, with great violence, all the air which is under them and cause a very strong wind, which does not last for long, which can be imitated if you stretch a sail out, just a little above the ground, and then let it fall flat against the earth.

Meteorology, II. VI, 312.

WISDOM, UNIVERSAL

Certainly it appears strange to me that so many people should investigate human customs with such care, the virtues of plants, the motions of the stars, the transmutations of metals, and the objects of similar sciences, while at the same time practically no one thinks about good understanding or universal wisdom.

Rules, I. X, 360.

WONDER

We naturally wonder more at the things which are above us than at those which are at the same height or below us.

Meteorology, I. VI, 231.

◈   ◈   ◈

When we first encounter some object which surprises us, and which we judge to be new, or quite different from what we knew previously, or from what we supposed it ought to be, this makes us wonder at it and be astonished at it. And because it can happen before we know in any way whether the object is useful to us, or whether it is not, it seems to me that wonder is the first of all the passions.

Passions, II, 53. XI, 373.

❖   ❖   ❖

Wonder is a sudden surprise of the soul, which causes it to turn to consider with attention the objects which seem rare and extraordinary to it.

Passions, II, 70. XI, 380.

WORDS

If several infants are raised together, they will not learn to talk all by themselves, except perhaps some words that they will invent, but which will not be either better or more proper than our own; on the contrary, our own words, which were invented at one time, have existed since that time, and are corrected and softened every day by our use of them, which does more, in such things, than a single great mind could do.

Letter to Mersenne, Mar. 4, 1630. I, 125-126.

❖   ❖   ❖

Who doubts that a Frenchman and a German have the same thoughts or reasonings concerning the same things, even though they conceive entirely different words?

Replies, III. IX, 139.

❖   ❖   ❖

Because we attach our conceptions to certain words, in order to express them through the mouth, and because we more often recall words than things, we can hardly conceive anything so distinctly that we entirely separate what we conceive from the words which have been chosen to express it. Thus everyone gives his attention to the words rather than to the things; which is the reason that they very frequently give their consent to terms that they do not understand.

Principles, I, 74. IX2, 60-61.

We see that words, whether spoken by mouth or written on paper, make the soul conceive all the things that they signify, and they, in turn, give it various passions.

Principles, IV, 197. IX2, 315-316.

◈ ◈ ◈

None of our external actions can give assurance to someone who examines them that our body is anything other than a machine which moves of itself, and which also has in it a soul which has thoughts, except the words or other signs which it makes, which are appropriate to the subjects which are presented to it, without relation to any passion.

Letter to Newcastle, Nov. 23, 1646. IV, 574.

◈ ◈ ◈

Although each movement of the [pineal] gland seems to have been joined by nature to each of our thoughts, from the beginning of our life, these movements may nevertheless be joined to other thoughts by habit: as experience shows that words, which excite movements in the gland which, according to the institution of nature, represent nothing to the soul other than their sound, when they are uttered by the voice, or by the shape of their letters, when they are written, and which, nevertheless, by the habit that has been acquired in thinking about what the words signify, when one has heard their sound or when one has seen their letters, customarily make one conceive the signification, rather than the shape of their letters or the sound of their syllables.

Passions, I, 50. XI, 368-369.

WORLD

This world, or the extended matter which composes the universe, has no limits, because, wherever we want to claim that they are, we can still imagine indefinitely extended spaces beyond them, which we do not merely imagine, but which we conceive to be actually as we imagine them.

Principles, I, 21. IX2, 74.

247